November 2006

THE Melbourne
BOOK
—— A history of now ——

OPPORTUNITY | SANCTUARY | PASSION | BEAUTY

Hardie Grant Books

MAREE COOTE

For Lex, Ginger, Bonny and everlasting George.

Published in 2003
by Hardie Grant Books
12 Claremont Street
South Yarra, Victoria 3141, Australia
www.hardiegrant.com.au

For a full list of picture credits see page 352

National Library of Australia Cataloguing-in-Publication Data:
Coote, Maree.
The Melbourne Book.

Bibliography.
Includes index.
ISBN 1 74066 049 8.

1. Melbourne (Vic.) - History. 2. Melbourne (Vic.) -Description and travel. I. Title.

994.51

Photography by Maree Coote
Cover and text design by Maree Coote
Printed and bound in China by SNP Leefung Printers

10 9 8 7 6 5 4 3 2

INTRODUCTION

Who could fall in love with Melbourne? How could it ever catch one's eye, let alone arouse one's passions? It's not New York, not Paris, not Prague. It's not shiny or pushy or loud. Melbourne is graceful and modest. And while it has stepped into its second century quietly and without much fanfare, its enduring modesty and quiet style have given rise to a thoroughly modern metropolis. This is truly Melbourne's time. It's simply the best place on earth to be born. The intelligent end of the lucky country, where thoughts run deeper, and passions are fiercely held. Melbourne. Voted the world's most liveable city. Traditional, green and gracious. Modern, smart and chic. And now that the world has noticed Melbourne, she is at risk of plunder, of global homogenisation, devaluing all that has brought her this far. The object of this book is both to protect and celebrate the best of Melbourne. It is a tribute to a unique original.

Little did I realise when I started to write this book that so many of the strands of Melbourne's history would intersect the way they do. I merely wondered as I walked down Swanston Street who Swanston was. And why I hadn't been taught the answer at school, along with a lot of other answers that were equally routine. I soon discovered that Batman first owned the blocks on which Myer now stands; Dames Melba and Edna both shopped for fashions at Le Louvre. Antoine Fauchery's 1852 bohemian adventure inspired Mirka Mora to her own adventure here 100 years later. Even Kylie echoes Melba's superstar turn from Melbourne to the top of the world.

Melbourne's story is unique in history. No other city has grown so fine so quickly. No other city is at once both the oldest continuously inhabited place on the globe and the youngest of cities. In a time and place warp, Melbourne's isolation from the rest of the world has encouraged a homegrown blend of tradition, innovation and diversity that is Melbourne's own unique language of style. From Vegemite to Ned Kelly, from the Botanic Gardens to Germaine Greer, Melbourne's creations are always in a league of their own.

I am no historian, just a curious city dweller in love with my place and time. Melbourne's stories ebb and flow across history, fading in and out of fashionable common knowledge. Facts change with curious regularity. History still hides as much as it reveals. Some stories sink in and out of the common awareness; others were never really there. Statues of Melbourne women are as scarce as Chinese footballers. The city's youthfulness means we still haven't got our own story straight. But it's early days. History has always been no more than the stories of the winners. But truth, as they say, is the daughter of time. And we've barely had any time at all, yet.

melbourne|victoria

Home of Australia's finest fashion | botani

gardens | government house | exhibition building

Birthplace of the world's only germain

greer | barry humphries | michael leunig | graham kennedy

phillip adams | **Home of Artists** norman lindsay | joh

brack | albert tucker | jan senbergs | joy hester | arthur boy

| fred williams | clifton pugh | mirka mora | fred mccubbin

sidney nolan | tom roberts | rupert bunny| arthur streeton

tommy maccrae | william barak | ellis rowan | margare

baskerville **Home to stars** cate blanchett | guy pearc

| kerry armstrong | vince colosimo | mary coustas | rache

griffiths | magda szubanski | kimberly davies | fred schepisi

gillian armstrong | **City of players** ted whitten | ro

barassi | roy cazaly | faith leech | peter thompson | rod laver

john bertrand | ron clarke | hubert opperman | gail couper

| roy higgins | bart cummings | bill ponsford | shane warne

Home of the world's first feature film | test cube baby | stock exchange | black box flight recorder **Home of the world's best** drinking water | **Home of the world's only** skyhooks | olivia newton-john | men@work | kylie | john farnham | seekers | renee geyer | tina arena | paul kelly | margaret roadknight | joe camilleri | nick cave | molly meldrum | daddy cool **Home of the world's richest** horse race | **Source of the world's only** vegemite | aspro | bionic ear | ute | cole's book arcade | **Place of legends** dame nellie melba | macpherson roberston | ethel 'henry handel' richardson | ned kelly | helena rubinstein | william buckley | percy grainger | percy cerutty | gough whitlam | edna walling | **Home of Australia's first** fairy floss | luna park | chewing gum | olympic games | impressionist artist | railway line | telephone exchange |

he's got more
front than myer's

been up and
down all day
like a swanston
street tram

four seasons in
one day

you've got tw
chances:
buckley's and
none

if you don't like
the weather
in melbourne,
wait a minute

the paris end c
collins street

contents

MELBOURNE

OPPORTUNITY | SANCTUARY | PASSION | BEAUTY

oppor

MELBOURNE

OPPORTUNITY | SANCTUARY | PASSION | BEAUTY

tunity

Picture the ancient, silent bush: so still that you ca[n] hear the sizzle of the heat haze, maybe the buzz of insec[ts] in the tea tree. Occupied for 40,000 years by the consta[nt] agenda of the Aboriginal balancing act of sustenance: t[he] present-minded focus on food and shelter for the here and now, manage[d] across an eternity by treading lightly on the earth. Into these centuries [of] isolation and reassuring predictability suddenly came 50 years of frenzy. [At] first passed over by colonial designers, this sweet bay haven w[as] discovered by canny squatters through the back door of Tasmania. In [a] matter of months the Aborigines had lost forever the precious relationsh[ip] with their place. It was transformed into a pretty pastoral hamlet whe[re] dour Scots and dull Englishmen fought petty squabbles over the spoils [of] stolen land upon which to graze their sheep. Politicking, posturing a[nd] prolonging the old prejudices of other places. But after 15 short years, [all] their powerplay was made into nonsense by the discovery of go[ld.] Overnight the hamlet was inundated by thousands upon thousands [of] Englishmen, Scots, Frenchmen, Germans, Austrians, Italian[s,] Californians, Chinese 'dragged from the ends of the earth by the irresistib[le] magnet of gold'. In the next 10 years the population increased 30-fold fro[m] 4500 to 140,000. A fundamental psychological shift occurred fro[m] controlled colony to New Frontier. Anything was possible in this land o[f a] new start. Many of the gold diggers were artisans and many, middle clas[s.] They were ethnically diverse. They brought radical thinking, bohemi[an]

festyles, Unionism, Chartism, Women's suffrage, Catholicism. They rought a new order to challenge the comfortable hierarchy of the first land arons. They challenged authority to the death at the Eureka Stockade in 854, in the name of building a democracy out of this colony. In the name f a fair go. In 10 years Victoria produced 20 million ounces of gold — one-hird of the world's total. The hamlet was already a city, endowing itself with he magnificent institutions of civilisation: libraries, universities, government uildings. Leap-frogging into a lifestyle other cities had waited hundreds of ears for. Participating in world commerce. Taking over from Sydney as ustralia's 'first' place. After the easy gold was won, the city settled into a nore measured rhythm. By the 1880s a new, powerful merchant class had stablished itself. There was plenty of money around. Up went Buckley & 'unn, grand hotels, the importers of Flinders Lane. Business and property oomed. Champagne flowed. More fine buildings were built. A grand life as created for many. Architects and builders thrived. Trams appeared. nternational exhibitions were held. Until just as suddenly — a fall in the wool rice, a financial hiccup in London, a run on the banks, and the boom was ver. The bust of 1893 emptied shop fronts, closed banks and filled the reets with unemployed. That left some powerful Haves, and thousands of ave-nots. It also left the larrikin character, radical inking, ethnic diversity, cultural variety, the demand for a ir go, and…trams. And Melbourne was born, in the pace of a single generation, ready for the 20th century.

timewarp

Named just 160 years ago, Melbourne is an infant compared to the other great cities of the world. Exploding from a city of tents to one of architectural grandeur, Melbourne became an international capital in the space of one single generation. This alone is a rare and remarkable occurrence, yet we have barely had the time to stop and think of what's been achieved in just 160 years. By contrast, Melbourne's Aboriginal timeline marks 40,000 years of the oldest continuously inhabited Aboriginal settlement in the country, and beyond 60,000 years of nomadic presence. In those terms, it's just moments since the first tall ships sailed into the bay. And because Melbourne's modern history is so short, it's easy to underrate it, even discard it in the face of newer, shinier times. Too few know the real story of Melbourne, and therein lies the risk: What we don't know is easy to lose.

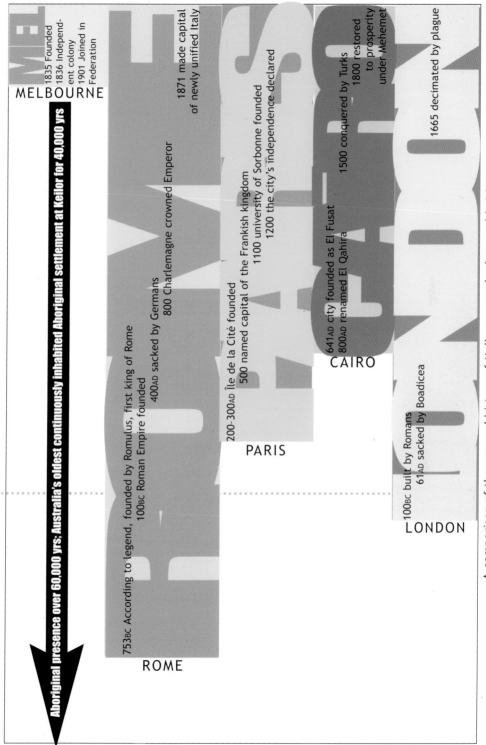

The following text appears within the timeline figure:

Timeline axis: BC1000 — 800 — 600 — 400 — 200 — BC·AD — 200 — 400 — 600 — 800 — 1000 — 1200 — 1400 — 1600 — 1800 — 2000AD

Aboriginal presence over 60,000 yrs: Australia's oldest continuously inhabited Aboriginal settlement at Keilor for 40,000 yrs

MELBOURNE
- 1835 Founded
- 1836 Independent colony
- 1901 Joined in Federation

ROME
- 753BC According to legend, founded by Romulus, first king of Rome
- 100BC Roman Empire founded
- 400AD sacked by Germans
- 800 Charlemagne crowned Emperor
- 1871 made capital of newly unified Italy

PARIS
- 200-300AD Île de la Cité founded
- 500 named capital of the Frankish kingdom
- 1100 university of Sorbonne founded
- 1200 the city's independence declared

CAIRO
- 641AD city founded as El Fusat
- 800AD renamed El Qahira
- 1500 conquered by Turks
- 1800 restored to prosperity under Mehemet

LONDON
- 100BC built by Romans
- 61AD sacked by Boadicea
- 1665 decimated by plague

A comparison of the age and history of Melbourne and other world cities.

7

whence melb

**melbourne
aka:
batmania
birr-arrung
bararing
bearbrass
bareheap
bareport
barrern
doutta galla
dutti-galla
glenelg
phillip**

Melbourne's Yarra River in 1886. The broad 'bay' section of the river formed a natural port and was the site of original Customs House. This was also where fresh river water met the seawater — the place known as 'the Fa

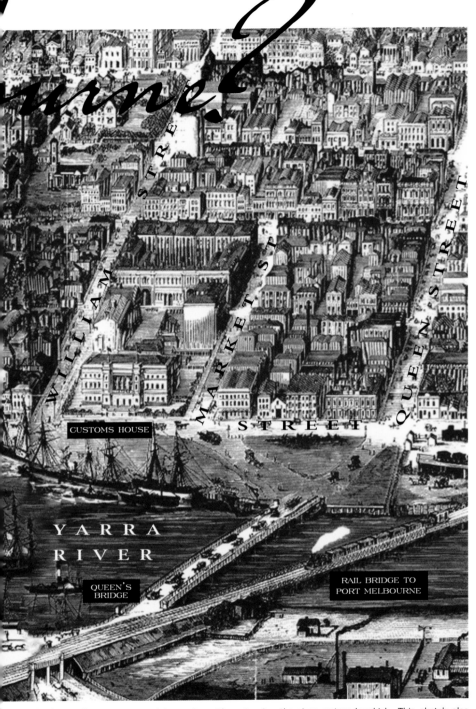

WILLIAM STREET

MARKET ST

QUEEN STREET

CUSTOMS HOUSE

STREET

YARRA
RIVER

QUEEN'S
BRIDGE

RAIL BRIDGE TO
PORT MELBOURNE

...til the dividing rocks were removed by early settlers, turning the river waters brackish. This sketch also ...ows Australia's first rail line and railbridge, built in 1854 by the Melbourne & Hobson's Bay Railway Company.

whence

LT GOV. DAVID
COLLINS
LANDED IN THE
WRONG PLACE,
AND PUT
MELBOURNE
OFF THE MAP
FOR CONVICTS.

Melbourne was never a convict settlement, and for that reason has enjoyed a sense of moral superiority over Sydney since its very beginning. But its origins are by no means untainted, despite the gloss of history books.

A combination of good luck and bad management kept convicts from settling Melbourne.

As the New South Wales settlement gradually consolidated, and Tasmania took its share of convicts, new locations for convict settlements were sought.

Lieutenant-Governor David Collins was sent to appraise Port Phillip, with a view to establishing a convict settlement there, based on glowing reports of Bass and Flinders who'd explored the area a few years earlier in 1799.

Collins' party set sail aboard *The Calcutta* and *The Ocean*. His group included 300 convicts, 16 married women, 50 royal marines and 15 settlers. However, he stopped just inside the heads, refusing to go any further into the bay, landing instead at the foot of Arthur's Seat at Sullivan Bay (Sorrento) in 1803.

Eleven-year-old John Pascoe Fawkner, his mother, sister and convict father were part of Collins' group, in search of a new home. Also aboard was William Buckley, a convict who soon escaped from Collins' settlement, disappearing into the bush without trace at Sorrento and creating a legend in his wake.

Unprepared to move further into the bay and tackle any natives without extra backup, Collins and his group endured their camp for seven months, desperate to be allowed to leave. With no freshwater source and dwindling provisions, Collins constantly lobbied his superiors to let him leave, declaring the area to be 'totally unfit for the purpose' of settlement. The freshwater Yarra River remained undiscovered to him, and his situation became untenable. His inaccurate and damning reports put Port Phillip Bay completely out of favour with the Sydney governors of the day. He was eventually allowed to depart for Tasmania, and so the convict settlers headed for Hobart instead.

And just as well. For had things gone to plan, a steady flow of convicts would have poured into Melbourne from then on, bringing a totally different and miserable beginning to European settlement instead of the lucky one she had instead.

Meanwhile, over the next several years other Europeans quietly enjoyed Port Phillip's arcadian aspect. A few settlers, explorers, and farmers meandered through or stayed. It was in fact an ideal spot to settle: temperate and green, with a broad harbour and the Yarra flowing through its heart laying up rich river soils. Tasmanian traders regularly visited Port Phillip Bay, and had been using the area as an illegal trading post since the early 1830s.

John Batman, a Tasmanian farmer, was the Australian-born son of a NSW convict. Batman gained fame in Tasmania for capturing the bushranger Matthew Brady. However, there is evidence that Batman was merely in the right place at the right time, after many others had spent months chasing the

BATMAN'S DEAL:
MELBOURNE
aka 'Duttigalla': 600,000 acres from Melbourne to Geelong

IN EXCHANGE FOR:
80 BLANKETS
42 TOMAHAWKS
130 KNIVES
250 HANDKERCHEIFS
62 PAIRS of SCISSORS
40 MIRRORS
150 lbs of FLOUR
18 SHIRTS
4 JACKETS
4 SUITS
Combined tally of two treaties, for Geelong and Melbourne

bushranger down. (Brady's gang was quite successful at evading and embarrassing the powers that be. When a reward was set for his capture, Brady posted a counter-reward for the capture of the Lieutenant-Governor of the day.)

Batman was also very active in the infamous 1830 Black Line Campaign of Tasmania, an offensive mounted to round up and capture as many as possible of the Tasmanian Aborigines.

Batman and others made regular visits from Tasmania. They eventually formed the Port Phillip Association, a collection of 13 Launceston farmers and traders who travelled to and from Port Phillip Bay for trade. The group charged Batman with the task of securing a spot to build a more permanent trading post township in the port, and he set sail from Tasmania aboard the *Rebecca* to find a site in 1835.

And so a now syphilitic Batman 'bought' 600,000 acres around what was to become Melbourne from the local Duttigalla Aborigines in exchange for scissors, beads, blankets, other goods and the promise of a yearly rent of similar content and value. For this he is popularly credited as being the founder of Melbourne.

Soon after, in 1835, some rough buildings

JOHN PASCOE FAWKNER
DESTINED FOR MELBOURNE EVER SINCE HIS FIRST VISIT IN 1803 ABOARD LT GOV. COLLINS' CONVICT SHIP. PORTRAIT BY WILLIAM STRUTT.

were erected by the 'Yarra Yarra' River, and Batman created a settlement which he called 'Bearbrass' — a curious misconstruction of one of the local Aboriginal names for the place, 'Bararing'.

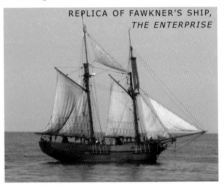

REPLICA OF FAWKNER'S SHIP, *THE ENTERPRISE*

John Pascoe Fawkner followed Batman across from Tasmania in his ship *The Enterprise* and set up camp near today's William Street. After a confrontation with Batman, some powerplay and posturing, the two rivals backed down and Fawkner moved to the other side of the river to Emerald Hill (South Melbourne). Their rivalry was to continue as they vied for premier position in the new town.

The rogue settlement of Port Phillip infuriated the Sydney authorities, but a year

He did the analysis.

TH FOR GRASS AND RICHNESS OF SOIL" BATMAN

JOHN BATMAN KEY AGENT OF THE
PORT PHILLIP ASSOCIATION.
LIVED JUST FOUR SHORT YEARS
IN THE MELBOURNE HE FOUNDED.

BATMAN AT THE SALE OF THE CENTURY

The purchase of 'Melbourne' from the Duttigalla people in 1835

whence

later in 1836 they decided it was easier to try to regulate the settlers — now numbering some 2000 — than fight them, and so they sent a police magistrate, William Lonsdale, down to keep an eye on the proceedings. The following year in 1837, they sent government surveyors Robert Hoddle and Robert Russell to design the town. Their work, a grid of streets and lanes that is both simple in design and simple to navigate, endures today as a model city framework.

Where Sydney had the meandering contours of the harbour to contend with, in Melbourne a grid of straight lines was created beside a conveniently straight stretch of river. Order and grace. Just like that. In Bearbrass, this pattern of wide, elegant streets was named for the British Kings and Queens of the day, with one for each of the key players and friends of Governor Bourke.

By 1837, the town was given its current name — Melbourne — after the British Prime Minister of the day, William Lamb, Lord Melbourne. And when in 1851 Victoria was created as a separate colony, Melbourne was named as its capital, and Charles La Trobe was installed as Governor.

John Batman died of syphilis in 1839 at just 38 years of age and was soon forgotten. (It wasn't until many years later that, in the 1935 Melbourne centenary celebrations, he was found worthy of commemoration.) In 1901, the year of Federation, Melbourne was named Australia's temporary capital, and remained so until 1927 when Canberra was founded.

Like so many histories, Melbourne's is one of luck, property barons, land grabs and fortune hunting. But thanks to Lt. Gov. Collins' unsuccessful visit, at least Melbourne was spared the inundation of a large, traumatised population of convicts and their accompanying miseries.

From the settlers' perspective at least, this comparatively gentler start, with its lack of convict history, followed by the discovery of gold, gave the city of Melbourne a dream beginning, a very rare thing indeed.

> Melbourne grew from a population of **50** in 1835 to **700,000** in 1869, the year of Fawkner's death.

HODDLE'S 1837 GRID OF STREETS, PLUS THE LATER ADDITION OF LATROBE STREET

LATROBE

LONSDALE

SPRING

STEPHEN

RUSSELL

SWANSTON

ELIZABETH

QUEEN

BOURKE

WILLIAM

COLLINS

KING

FLINDERS

SPENCER

PRINCE'S BRIDGE

river

Yarra Yarra

Yarra

BATMAN'S HILL

EMERALD HILL
ALSO KNOWN AS CANVASTOWN

FAWKNER'S TERRITORY
BOUNDARIED BY
PICKLES ST, CITY RD,
GRANT ST AND
CLARENDON ST.

Bearbrass

Williamstown

Fishermans Bend

Sandridge
(FORMERLY LIARDET'S BEACH 1839)

PORT PHILLIP BAY

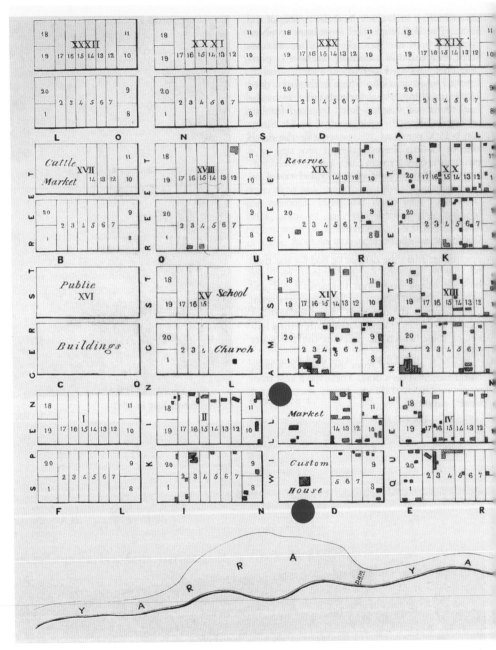

This map details the real estate allotments of early Melbourne. Two of these lots, corner allotments bounded by Collins and William streets, were the subject of a bitter bidding duel by founding rivals Batman and Fawkner. The map also shows the original two blocks in Bourke Street bought by Batman in 1838 that are today the home of Myer

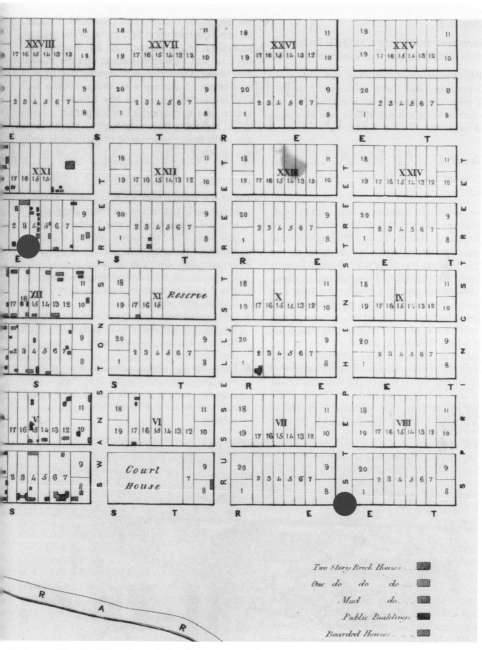

Melbourne. Here, Exhibition Street is listed as 'Stephen Street', its original name. This map also marks the Custom House site, which was one of the first huts built; it was later rebuilt to last, and still stands today at the corner of Williams and Flinders streets opposite Melbourne's first harbour and the dam known as 'the Falls'.

NORTH–SOUTH STREETS

SPENCER

Sources differ, suggesting Spencer, Lord Althorpe of the Melbourne Club, or alternately Governor Bourke's great friend the English politician John Charles Spencer.

Phillip Gidley **KING**
Third Governor of NSW.

WILLIAM

After King William IV.

QUEEN

After King William's consort, Queen Adelaide.

ELIZABETH

Probably after 'The Virgin Queen' herself, but Hoddle maintained it was a dedication by Governor Bourke for his own daughter, Elizabeth.

Captain Charles **SWANSTON**

Swanston was an East India Company man. He arrived in Hobart in 1831, took up a position as Chairman of the Derwent Bank and introduced the 'overdraft' to Australia. As the chairman of the Port Phillip Association, he was the architect of Batman's quest. Governor Bourke insisted a street be named for him.

RUSSELL

Sources differ, suggesting Earl Russell, or alternately the British ex-Prime Minister Lord John Russell.

EXHIBITION / STEPHEN

Originally named Stephen St, after the Under-Secretary of State for the Colonies, until 1888 when it was renamed for the great Centennial Exhibition of Melbourne. Modelled on the famous English and French Expos, these promotional inter-colonial get-togethers were an aid to investment, commerce and entertainment. They were regular events on the calendar between 1864 and 1900.

SPRING

A puzzle of history, it is so named either for the fragrant charm of wattles and flowering gums in season at the time of naming, or as a tribute to Bourke's great friend, Thomas Spring Rice, later to become Lord Monteagle. The 'underground spring' notion favoured by some is, it seems, no more than a myth.

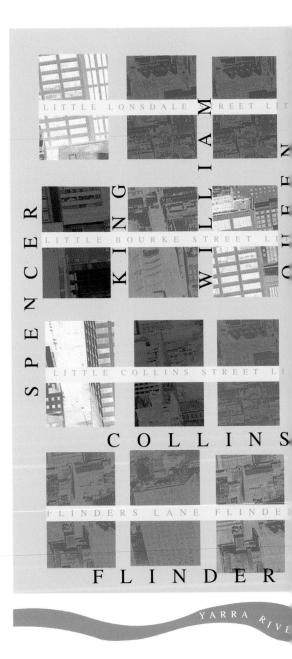

EAST–WEST STREETS

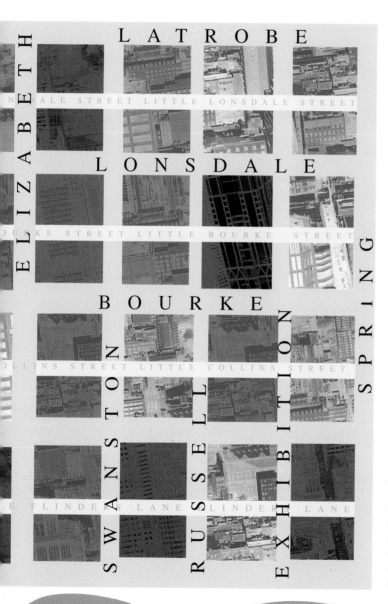

LA TROBE, Charles Joseph 1801–75
First Superintendent of the Port Phillip
District, and later first Governor of
Victoria. La Trobe added this street to
Hoddle's original grid in 1839, and
named it after himself.

LONSDALE, Captain William 1799–1864
First Police Magistrate of Melbourne, and
first Victorian Colonial Secretary.

BOURKE, Sir Richard 1777–1855
Governor of the colony of NSW and
therefore Governor of Melbourne until
separation. Bourke was a liberal thinker
who moved to allow ex-convicts into jury
service, to limit the power of magistrates,
and to create a national system of
education instead of funding church
schools.

COLLINS, Lieutenant-Governor David
1756–1810
Commander of the misdirected convict
settlement of 1803, landing in Sorrento,
instead of Melbourne. His unfavourable
reports prevented Melbourne from ever
receiving convict settlement. Collins was
also a valued legal mind in the NSW
colony, and writer of a sympathetic
account of the Aborigines and the harm
done to them by white settlement.

FLINDERS, Matthew 1774–1814
English navigator. Sailed with George
Bass aboard the *Tom Thumb*, and
together they mapped the Victorian
coastline in detail, discovering Bass
Strait.

PAINTINGS BY MELBOURNE ARTIST JAN SENBERGS SHOW THE FIGURE OF BUCKLEY IN THE LANDSCAPE AROUND THE BELLARINE PENINSULA AND AIREY'S INLET, DRESSED IN HIS ABORIGINAL ACCOUTREMENTS, ALONG WITH HIS SYMBOLIC TALL HAT AND POINTED BEARD.

SENBERGS PREFERS THE BUCKLEY TALE EVEN TO THAT OF NED KELLY. " IT'S A TERRIFIC THEME TO HAVE – FAR MORE POWERFUL THAN THE KELLY THEME, BUCKLEY'S STORY GOES ACROSS CULTURES... IT'S A MUCH MORE MEANINGFUL, MORE SIGNIFICANT THING."   ARTWORK 'BUCKLEY'S CAVE' BY JAN SENBERGS 1996

BUCKLEY

William Buckley

The wild white man
of Melbourne

"put 'im down
black fellow,
jump up white fellow"

Buckley's story has all the hallmarks that great legends require: big stature, big character, big adventure and big concepts at its very centre: justice, slavery, racism, man against nature. This is a rare tale of the successful castaway. Robinson Crusoe was a fiction. Buckley was real. But the easy temptation to romanticise his story is constantly challenged by Buckley's own unique humanity — unsure, brave, frightened, lonely and loyal. It is a study in the capacity we all possess to adapt and accept, in both thought and deed.

William Buckley was born in Cheshire, England, in 1780, and raised by his grandparents. They educated him and taught him a trade, until this turbulent young man joined the army at the age of 19. He fought for Britain in Holland against Napoleon's French republicans in 1800 where he was seriously wounded in the right hand. He returned to an impoverished London that offered him little opportunity. After stealing a bolt of fabric with some mates, he was convicted and sentenced to a prison work party.

After six months, Buckley, being skilled as a bricklayer and mechanic, was selected for 'transportation for life' as a potentially useful member of the first attempt to create a penal colony in Port Phillip.

Buckley left England in April 1803, aboard

They called him Murrangurk — One who has been reincarnated.

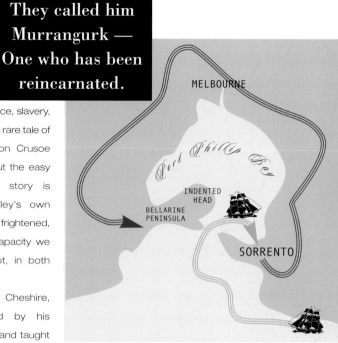

Lieutenant-Governor Collins' convict ship *Calcutta* which landed in Sorrento on 19 October.

After three months of labouring to establish the colony, Buckley and three others escaped on Christmas Eve.

'The attempt was little short of madness, for there was before me the chances of being retaken, and probable death,...or starvation in an unknown country inhabited by savages...These perils...were then staring me in the face; but possessed of great personal strength, and good constitution,...I determined on braving everything and, if possible, making my escape.'

ALL EXCERPTS FROM JOHN MORGAN, *THE LIFE AND ADVENTURES OF WILLIAM BUCKLEY* 1852 REPRODUCED BY ARES BOOKS 1996

19 convicts escaped from Sorrento: 13 were recaptured or returned, and six were never heard from again.

Of the four escapees, one was shot as the others disappeared into the bush. They headed north in the hope of finding Sydney, planning to lose themselves in the busy city throng.

But they soon lost their course, and instead, rounded the bay until they reached the Bellarine Peninsula on the other side. From there they could see the settlement they had left, just across the bay. Realising their mistaken direction Buckley's two companions were horrified, and so, exhausted and mentally beaten, decided to turn back and give themselves up rather than die in the bush. One made it back, one did not. Buckley opted to continue on, alone and distraught.

'When I had parted from my companions, although I had preferred doing so, I was overwhelmed with the various feelings which oppressed me...I thought of friends, of my youth, the scenes of my boyhood, and early manhood, of the slavery of my punishment, of the liberty I had panted for, which although now realised made my heart sick, even at its enjoyment. I was here subjected to the most severe mental sufferings for several hours and then pursued my solitary journey.'

Buckley's path from his home in Cheshire, to war in Holland, to imprisonment in London, transportation to Port Phillip and ultimately life as a castaway at only 23 years of age takes us to just the beginning of his remarkable story.

Buckley was embarking on life's most extreme challenge: alone in an unknown land, man against nature, for the next 32 years.

'I look back at that period of my life with inexpressible astonishment, considering it altogether a dreaming delusion and not reality.'

Buckley lived wandering the landscape, and holed up in a cave for a time, near Anglesea. He survived precariously on abalone and berries. He suffered from starvation and weakness until he found water, shellfish and 'luxurious living' at Airey's Inlet, moving on after a week to Mt Defiance where he remained for several months. There: 'I fared sumptuously every day, and rapidly recovered my strength, mentally and bodily. I remember a fancy coming over me that I could have remained at that spot all the rest of my life...but it was never intended that man should live alone...so implanted in his nature are social feelings and yearnings for society...'

Buckley had had some brief encounters with Aborigines up to this time, but nothing enduring. Overcome by loneliness, he eventually resolved to return to his ship (long since gone, the settlement having been abandoned in favour of Hobart).

He set off back the way he had come approximately a year before. Living hand to mouth as he travelled he grew dangerously weak from lack of food. He found and kept a spear from an Aboriginal burial mound to use as a walking stick. Later, collapsing desolate and exhausted, he was found by two Warthaurong women who mistook him for the reincarnation of the previous owner of the spear, one of their own warriors. Elated, the tribe adopted him as one

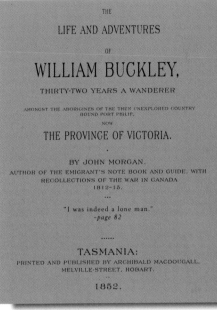

THE

LIFE AND ADVENTURES

OF

WILLIAM BUCKLEY,

THIRTY-TWO YEARS A WANDERER

AMONGST THE ABORIGINES OF THE THEN UNEXPLORED COUNTRY
ROUND PORT PHILIP,

NOW

THE PROVINCE OF VICTORIA.

BY JOHN MORGAN,

AUTHOR OF THE EMIGRANT'S NOTE BOOK AND GUIDE, WITH
RECOLLECTIONS OF THE WAR IN CANADA
1812-15.

"I was indeed a lone man."
-*page 82*

TASMANIA:

PRINTED AND PUBLISHED BY ARCHIBALD MACDOUGALL,
MELVILLE-STREET, HOBART.

1852.

of their own, returned from the dead. Buckley's imposing figure — six foot six inches tall and tattooed — adequately fulfilled the mythology of a ghostly, pale spirit figure returned from 'Skyland'.

Buckley's story of his time living with the Aborigines was later told in his autobiography, *The Life and Adventures of William Buckley*, written in 1852 with the help of Tasmanian journalist John Morgan when Buckley was 70 years old. These fascinating memoirs document this time living with the Warthaurong people as one both of great community and of immense isolation. The violent and sickening regularity of tribal wars over women, possessions and honour disturbed Buckley greatly.

He led a charmed existence, however, never being personally involved in any of these struggles. But witnessing their bloody detail, including some cannibalism and eventually the tragic loss of his closest tribal relatives, ultimately led him after 25 years to leave the group and live alone.

> **"The whole affair was in ct a species of madness."**
> **William Buckley**

He built himself a daub and stick house on the Karaaf River (Bream Creek at Breamlea, near Barwon Heads). He set up permanent fish traps, and survived well on yams and fish. He lived for some years in solitary peace, visited now and then by passing tribes.

Eventually, Buckley heard of trouble brewing. Natives had met with white men (Batman's party) at a beach camp at Indented Head, and were plotting to muster some numbers and then return to kill and rob the visitors. Buckley decided to intervene, both in order to mediate, and to re-encounter his own people.

And so in 1835, 32 years after his escape, Buckley strolled out of the bush at Indented Head, dressed in kangaroo hides and sporting a massive beard, to greet his countrymen. These were Batman's men including Henry Batman, John Batman's brother, left behind to hold a presence while John Batman sped his prized Melbourne 'treaty' back to Launceston.

Buckley's re-introduction to his own people was a culture shock. He struggled to get his language back after 30 years of non-use. He was so fluent in the local Aboriginal tongue that the Governor's men granted him an immediate pardon and hired him as their interpreter at a salary of £50. He operated as go-between and peace-keeper. But he grew increasingly dismayed at the treatment of the Aborigines by the settlers, and less and less comfortable with their politics and his role as their intermediary.

Buckley eventually became totally disenchanted with the settlers and their often violent tactics, becoming sullen and uncooperative. He quit the service of the government after two years' work as interpreter and left Melbourne for Hobart, where he married, and lived until his death in 1856 aged 76.

Around 1850, Buckley applied for a modest pension due to him as an ex-public servant — indeed Melbourne's first ever public servant — but it was John Pascoe Fawkner, now an influential publican, publisher and civic 'father', who complained that Buckley was undeserving, that he had been too reluctant to aid in the capture and conviction of Aborigines. Nonetheless Buckley won out, perhaps helped by the rising interest in his recently published memoirs.

Buckley and Fawkner had both come to Port Phillip on the same ship with Lt Gov. Collins in 1803 — Buckley as a 23-year-old convict, and Fawkner as an 11-year-old boy with his convict father. One eventually called himself the 'father' of Melbourne. The other may well be called Melbourne's first father of Reconciliation.

The expressions
You've got Buckley's hope
or *Buckley's chance* refer to the
estimation of Buckley's chances of
survival in the bush alone after his
escape: No chance.
The later expression *You've got two
chances: Buckley's and none*
incorporates a new name on the
Melbourne city scene – Buckley & Nunn
Bourke Street Emporium of 1852
– into a mixed and more emphatic
expression of having both
No chance <u>and</u> None.
Hindsight reveals Buckley was
in fact one of the luckiest
characters in history.

By the beginning of 15th century, the Europeans had advanced their technologies to such a degree that they found themselves able to push out into the world — a world that had kept pretty much to itself.

Masters of technology and invention, they had developed ships and navigational instruments to take them far. They had perfected warfare and weaponry to subdue opposition, and mastered writing to spread ideas, information, and doctrine over time and distance. And they had learned how to preserve foods — a simple yet fundamental advance that freed them for other exploits. These were powerful skills, all of which made the world open up to Europe like an oyster.

By the 18th century, one last frontier beckoned irresistibly to the European adventurer. The unknown and remote land downunder, *terra australis*, had remained isolated from the rest of the world since the end of the ancient ice ages, when seas began to rise and landscapes changed forever. Australian Aborigines had existed here successfully in isolation for at least 40,000 years.

Of all nature's creatures, only man does not adapt to his environment, instead changing the environment to suit his need.

Not so the Aborigine.

Australian Aborigines had developed a complex lifestyle based on an intimate knowledge of the environment that allowed a sustained and measured existence. An acute understanding of seasonal, geographical and botanical phenomena combined with a respect for the balance between land and inhabitant ensured a sustainable lifestyle in a difficult environment.

This ability to read the environment was the key to survival. The first blossoms of tea tree signalled the season's first batch of swan's eggs. Landscape, season, fire, drought, every aspect of the environment held the secrets of food and shelter for those who'd learned to read the signs. The Aboriginal lifestyle was one of subtle interaction with the land, of abstract concepts of land and animal custodianship, of community, of belonging, and of intricate sharing systems.

William Buckley tells of seeing tribesmen wailing in deep dismay at the lack of another tribe with whom to share an unusually large find of tortoise eggs. Nature's bounty was so highly regarded, it was never taken for granted, and waste was seen as both travesty and tragedy.

But their need to hunt and gather every day kept the Aborigines tied to a survival routine that occupied their entire consciousness. So while the Australian Aborigine was locked so closely into nature's cycles, the European was freed to roam, often trampling nature underfoot.

It is not surprising then that the British could only see Australia as useful or useless, farmland or wasteland, while the Aborigines saw their very existence in every stone and leaf. The resultant collision of these two polar attitudes was inevitably tragic. One so powerful, with little sensitivity to anything but progress, and the other powerless, with little means with which to articulate or protect its own value.

Surely no two groups could have better complemented each other's knowledge, but in the ignorance of the 19th century it was not to be, and in a few short years the centuries-old harmony of Aboriginal life had changed forever.

"They held that the bush and all it contains are man's general property, that private property is only what utensils are carried in the bag; and this general claim to nature's bounty extends even to the success of the day; hence at the close, those who have been successful divide with those who have not been so. There is no 'complaining in the streets' of a native encampment; none lacketh while others have it; nor is the gift considered as a favour but a right brought to the needy, and thrown down at his feet."

William Thomas describes the balance of Aboriginal society
in his *Brief Account of the Aborigines of Australia Felix*
quoted in T.F. Bride's *Letters from Victorian Pioneers*, 1898

Original Title: Blackfellow Painted for a Corroboree
Photograph by Antoine Fauchery, from his *Sun Pictures of Victoria*,1858
La Trobe Picture Collection, State Library of Victoria

ABORIGI

The Aboriginal presence in the Melbourne area dates back more than 40,000 years. Keilor is reputed to be the oldest continuously occupied site in the whole of Australia. Tasmania was once connected to the mainland, and the bay was a vast dry plain, where early Aborigines enjoyed plentiful kangaroo hunting. Generations of Melbourne's Aborigines watched the birth of Port Phillip Bay as, slowly but surely, it was formed by rising seas around 9,000 years ago.

The original inhabitants of 'Melbourne' were the Kulin nation, which comprised a number of tribal groups. Of these, a clan now thought to be the Kurnaje-berring (also known as Wurundjeri or, by their language, Woiworong) were called the 'Duttigalla tribe' by Batman. They lived in the Yarra area and were those with whom Batman struck his deal in 1835.

Batman produced two treaties, one for Melbourne, and one for Geelong. He put the signatures of the same Aborigines to both, when in fact the custodianship of these vastly different areas was held by at least five different tribes — the Wathaurong, Kurung, Woiworong, Bunurong and Taungurong.

TRIBES AND REGIONS

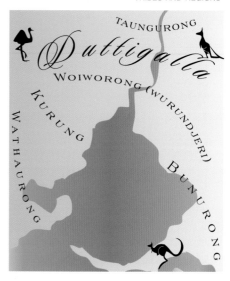

Batman's 'treaty' records eight names as signatories although they all seem to be incorrect. They were listed as Cooloolock, Bungarie, Yanyan, Moowhip, Mommarlalar, and three others all given the same name — Jagajaga. Bungarie is the name of a well-known Sydney Aborigine, not a party to this treaty. It is now believed Billebellary, a leader of the Kurnaje-berring was present, although he is not mentioned in the treaty at all.

Needless to say, Batman's treaty was a farce in more ways than one. The signatories understood nothing of the document's contents. The Aboriginal interpreters Batman had brought along were from NSW and did not speak the local languages.

It is likely and logical these signatories thought the signing of the paper itself resulted in the payment of goods, and did not know it to be a symbol for the abstract land transfer that signing represented to the white settlers. And it is now known that Aborigines at this meeting would have understood that tribal land is sacred and can never be disposed of. The act of sale of land is fundamentally contrary to their lore.

In the minds of the white settlers, however, the deal was done, and they began to inhabit the area very quickly thereafter. The deal infuriated the authorities in Sydney because by its very nature it acknowledged proprietorship of land by the Aborigines — a notion the Crown would not allow, claiming this land had no owners — that it was *terra nullius*, 'unoccupied land'. The Crown very quickly took control of the settlement, forcing Batman and his cronies to bid and pay for land at auction like any other settler.

At first fed and encouraged into friendship, many Aborigines relaxed into the relationship with settlers. As building and development grew, however, they were pushed back into the bush and away from water and fishing resources, from lands they had hunted for centuries until eventually both food and friendship were withdrawn.

By the time Batman arrived in Port Phillip in 1835, the Aboriginal population had been all but wiped out from Tasmania, a task in which Batman himself had played a major role. In Melbourne too, the Aborigines were variously shunned, hunted or enslaved. They often fought back, or stole supplies. Described once as 'the greatest drawback to emigration' plans were eventually activated on all frontiers of settlement to eradicate them. The first hangings at Melbourne Gaol were of Aboriginal men known as 'Bob' and 'Jack', hung for the murder of two sailors at Westernport.

Know all Persons that We Three

Bungarie, Yanyan, c[...]

being the Chiefs of a certain N[...]

by us The above Mentioned Chiefs Framoo   being possessed of the

Tomahawks, One Hundred Knives, Fifty Pair of Scissors, Thirty Looki[...]

delivered to us by John Batman residing in Va[...]

Heirs and Successors **Give** Grant Enfeoff and confirm unto the said Joh[...]

from the branch of the River at the top of the Port, about 7 Miles from the

Downs or Plains and from thence South, South West across Mount Vilaum[...]

and containing about Five Hundred Thousand more acres as the same hath b[...]

by certain marks made upon the Trees growing along the boundaries of the

To the Use of the said John Batman his heirs and Assigns for ever

said tract of Land and place thereon Sheep and Cattle **Victoria**

Blankets, One Hundred Knives, One Hundred Tomahawks, Fifty Sui[...]

whereof We Jagajaga, Jagajaga, Jagajaga, the above mentioned Princes[...]

the said Tribe have hereunto affixed our Seals to these presents and have

One thousand eight hundred and thirty five

Signed Sealed and Delivered in the presence of Us the same having
been fully and properly interpreted and explained to the said Chiefs

James Gumm

Alexander Thompson

Willm Todd

Signed on the Banks of Batman's Creek
6th June 1835

34

Jagajaga, Jagajaga, Jagajaga, being the Principal Chiefs and also Cooloolock
nd Mommarmalar

called Dutigallar situate at and near Port Phillip, Called

hereinafter mentioned for and in consideration of Twenty Pair of Blankets, Thirty

Two Hundred Handkerchiefs, and One Hundred Pounds of Flour, and Six Shirts

Land Esquire but at present sojourning with us and our Tribe DO for ourselves our

his heirs and assigns **All That** tract of Country situate and being at Port Phillip, Running

he River, Forty Miles North East and from thence — West Forty Miles across Iramoo
along Harbour at the head of the same

execution of these presents delineated and marked out by Us according to the custom of our Tribe

Land **To Hold** the said Tract of Land with all advantages belonging thereto unto and

tent that the said John Batman his heirs and assigns may occupy and possess the

g to Us and our heirs or successors the yearly Rent or Tribute of One Hundred Pair of

, Fifty Looking glasses, Fifty Pair Scissors and Five tons Flour **In Witness**

, and Cooloolock, Bungarie, Yanyan, Moowhip & Mommarmalar the Chiefs of

same Date according to the Christian Era this Sixth day of June

Jagajaga his mark

Jagajaga his mark

Jagajaga his mark

Cooloolock his mark

Bungarie his mark

Yanyan his mark

Moowhip his mark

Mommarmalar his mark

John Batman

BATMAN'S 'MELBOURNE' DEED, ONE OF THE TWO (ONE FOR MELBOURNE, ONE FOR GEELONG) DRAWN UP BY GELLIBRAND IN TASMANIA BEFORE BATMAN'S EXPEDITION. LA TROBE AUSTRALIAN MANUSCRIPTS COLLECTION, STATE LIBRARY OF VICTORIA

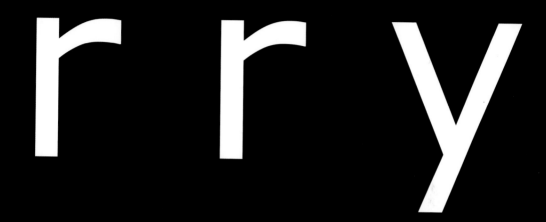

r r y

"THE PAST IS NEVER FULLY GONE.
IT IS ABSORBED INTO THE PRESENT AND THE FUTURE.
IT STAYS TO SHAPE WHAT WE ARE AND WHAT WE DO."
Sir William Deane, Governor-General, Inaugural Vincent Lingiari Memorial Lecture, 1996

tommy mccrae

(c. 1836–1901)

Tommy McCrae was more than a gifted Aboriginal artist. He was a unique historian.

A member of the Pangerang tribe (also known as the KwatKwat), Tommy McCrae's family settled around Lake Moodemere near Wahgunyah by the Murray River.

Like most Aboriginal artists, McCrae painted and drew scenes of significant events within Aboriginal society. Nothing new there. The tradition of recording events in mud and stick was a common pastime. But in 1858 his skill was noticed by the Wahgunyah postmaster, Mr Kilborn, who gave Tommy paper, ink and encouragement. And so instead of drawing on rocks or in mud, Tommy McCrae worked on white man's paper, in pen and ink. This brought his art to a much broader audience, one that was unlikely to seek out Aboriginal artistic expression in caves in the bush.

His art was portable, collectible and popular. This made McCrae's artistic career viable and gave his illustrated chronicles of Melbourne a real presence among other histories.

His stories are an eloquent telling of the major events including those in Melbourne, seen from the black perspective. He recorded important scenes of Aboriginal life — corroborees, ceremonies, famous hunts, fights, foreign invasions and other historic events. Like the story of William Buckley — the wild white man of Melbourne — a story that came to light when McCrae was a mere infant. In this we can see McCrae the historian, telling and retelling stories beyond those of his place. The names of his sketches also reveal his historic focus, in titles like *Melbourne tribe when blacks saw ship first*, *Echuca blacks in old times*, *Sydney tribe in olden times* and *Buckley ran away from the ship*.

McCrae's style was typical of many cave drawings — graphic silhouettes of figures and animals, and minimalistic landscapes, all strikingly expressive for their economy of line, and enhanced by the strong black and white contrast of his medium. Often, figures were arranged in a frieze, emphasising the graphic shapes through this repetition.

Curiously, McCrae's method was to start drawing at the bottom of the page and work up. Each drawing began by establishing the ground on which the scene would take place. He would draw the boots, and then the feet and legs of figures or animals, the base of tree trunks, finishing off at the topmost leaf.

He made hundreds of sketches and earned a living all his life from his art. He recorded the intersection of Aboriginal life with new worlds, his often humorous observations portraying foreigners as ridiculous figures. White fashions, ship design, Chinese "coolies" — were all rendered with a masterly skill for expression, from an eye well trained in the acute observation of animal behaviour.

Tommy McCrae's black perspective captured on white paper is a rare and valuable treasure. He sold a sketchbook for 10 shillings in 1889. Another brought $300,000 at sale by Sotheby's in 2001. Modern, eloquent, witty, McCrae's works are today recognised as masterpieces of history and art.

Aborigines Chasing Chinese; Hunting Scene TOMMY McCRAE, MUSEUM OF VICTORIA

Lachlan War Dance TOMMY McCRAE, LA TROBE COLLECTION, STATE LIBRARY OF VICTORIA

Buckley Ran Away from the Ship, Tommy McCrae c.1870 Koorie Heritage Trust Inc Collection, Victoria

When Mirka Mora was just a girl of 16 in Paris, she peeked into the pages of what was then considered a saucy book, written in 1857 by Henri Murger, called *Scenes de la Vie Bohème*. It was a kind of soap opera of its day, describing the exploits of a group of 'Beautiful People' in Paris as they lived and loved their exotic lives. Eventually the story became an opera — *La Bohème*. The character of the great lover, Marcel, was based on the author's companion, a young man named Antoine Fauchery.

Fauchery was an artist, adventurer, engraver, writer and photographer, who among other exploits, travelled to Melbourne in 1852 to find his fortune on the goldfields. Although the goldfields let him down, he achieved many other things, including opening an intimate and cosmopolitan café in Little Bourke Street, creating a series of legendary photographs, and writing a unique account of his visit to Melbourne called *Lettres d'un Mineur en Australie*. He kept the company of artists, writers, musicians and high society. He carved himself a reputation and a career or two, and returned to Paris filled with tall tales and true. His life rang out loud with creative freedom and possibility, and was a great inspiration to Mora.

THE INSPIRATIONAL
ANTOINE FAUCHERY.

In 1951, recalling the Fauchery connection, Mirka convinced husband Georges Mora to choose Melbourne from the three possible locations in which he was offered work that year: Casablanca, Saigon and Melbourne. And so, like Fauchery, Mora also brought to Melbourne an insatiable creative talent, passion, energy and great coffee. She created her own *vie bohème* beginning with the Mirka Café, the Contemporary Art Society of Melbourne, first the Balzac then the Tolarno restaurants, Tolarno Galleries and myriad other creative projects. Ever the coquette, Mora is unstoppable. Her modus operandi echoes that of Musetta, the darling of *Scenes de la Vie Bohème*' who was '...intelligent, shrewd, and above all hostile to anything that she considered tyranny: she had but one rule: Caprice.'

"In 1951 the choice for me was Casablanca, Saigon or Melbourne."

PHOTO BY GEOFFREY SMITH

mirka mora   artist

"Between Melbon and Sydnee, zere was a leetle rivalry. Melbon 'ad ze best painters, I mean we 'ad Sydnay Nolan, Joy 'Ester, Boyd, Tucker, Perceval... Eez good to 'ave a leetle rivalry."

"Ah 'ad ze idée fix in my 'ead to go to Melbon, and Ah don regret it."
Mirka Mora

As French adventurer Antoine Fauchery sailed into Melbourne in 1852 he was struck by the lack of variety among the ships moored there. An experienced traveller, he was skilled at recognising ships — '...*the American by the dizzy height of the masts on his clippers; the Dutchman by his thick-necked three-masters; the Chinaman by the extravagant shape of his junks...and the Frenchman by my own heartbeats...*' but in Melbourne, as his eyes scanned the port '...*all that is missing. Here there are only huge black vessels, at the stern of which you read LONDON or*

A FRENCH PERSPECTIVE
Antoine Fauchery

After the often dull documents of the historic record, the account of Melbourne written by Parisian artist, writer and adventurer Antoine Fauchery is a welcome change. Considered a celebrity in France, this dashing member of Paris' most darling bohemian set sailed to Melbourne in 1852, looking to make his fortune on the goldfields. When he returned to Paris after four years, Fauchery wrote an account of his time in Melbourne entitled *Lettres d'un Mineur en Australie*, an unusually evocative view of Melbourne that displays a truly different vantage point — that of a genuine man of the world. His words lack the stuffiness and vested interests of early British accounts. Indeed he was reviewing the British presence just as much as he was the Melbourne frontier. Full of creative scrutiny, bemused horror, disappointment and genuine surprise, *Lettres* conjures a Melbourne of great wonder and interest.

Fauchery tried for 22 months to strike it lucky in the goldfields. Unsuccessful, he gave up and returned to Melbourne with his last £60. There he opened the 'Café Estaminet Français' (little French port) at 76 Little Bourke Street. Here he created a cultured port in a barbaric colonial storm, catering to European emigrants who 'lacked any sort of social milieu and sought in vain a little corner where they could sit in comfort.' And very soon 'my house had become the rendezvous for all foreigners.'

His café flourished for just four short months, when the effects of the Eureka Stockade caused an economic crisis that dried up his custom. He returned to the goldfields to earn enough for his return fare to London in 1856.

After writing *Lettres*, Fauchery returned to Melbourne the following year with his new wife. He established himself as a photographer in Collins Street, and created his famous *Sun Pictures of Victoria*, a series he produced in collaboration with another miner/photographer, Richard Daintree. This series contains some of the most striking and rare images of Aborigines and miners from that time. He went on to further travels in Manila and China, and eventually to Japan in 1861 where he died just three months after his arrival from gastritis and dysentery.

ANTOINE FAUCHERY

Fauchery brought his stylish gaze and his talent to create some of the greatest written and photographic essays on early Melbourne, inspiring many others — including Mirka Mora over 100 years later — to do the same.

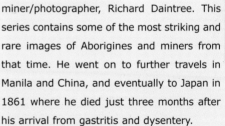

Work prospects *"If only I could cook! Instead of bringing Rabelais and Montaigne with me, if I had simply brought* The Country House *or* The Middle-class Housewife, *I could at this moment, turn out stews, gravies and sauces at the Black Bull Hotel where they are offering 500 francs a week for a French cook!"*

Bushrangers *"But there is also the question of bushrangers who infest the town and country for thirty m[?] around. The bushranger, according to the portrait of him that is painted for us, is nothing less than a well-ni[?] fabulous being, a red-bearded ruffian with sharp pointed teeth and no end of pistols, who plunders everybod[?] indiscriminately. These details make the ladies shudder, and even more so their husbands…"*

On the lack of available accommodation *"In fifteen minutes, I counted fourteen buildings dominating [?] town, all fourteen of them churches. It would be a sorry state of affairs if in a country where the good Lord has so many dwellings, some of His creatures had to sleep in the street."*

A comparison between London and Melbourne *"[London]… The largest city in the world! That… leaves a gap that irritates Melbourne people somewhat, but they console themselves for it by swearing St George, drinking gin and becoming millionaires."*

Landscape *"The Land… Alas, it is very dismal, the part that runs to the right and left of the Yara-Yara! consists of vast plains slightly undulating… Plains, and then more plains, stretching out* ad infinitum, *like the boredom that comes over you at the sight of them. It lacks the power to surprise or move you, and does not even have in its favour the heartbreak there is in sterility."*

Architecture *"Whereas I had expected to find wooden houses, huts even, hastily erected and scattered among the trees, I found houses of one or two storeys, solidly built, aligned as straight as a die, forming str[?] a kilometre long, very straight, very wide, perfectly macadamised, and in these streets, black coats, collars, sil[?] dresses, heeled boots, everything just as Europe…"*

Extracts from *Lettres d'un Mineur en Australie* by Antoine Fauchery, translated from the French by A.R.Chisol[?]

MELBOURNE IS MADE OUT OF GOLD.

MORE THAN £100 MILLION WORTH OF GOLD
WAS UNEARTHED IN AUSTRALIA IN THE 1850S.

OVER 90% OF AUSTRALIA'S GOLD IN THAT TIME
CAME FROM VICTORIA.

VICTORIA PRODUCED 20 MILLION OUNCES OF GOLD BETWEEN
1851 AND 1860 — ONE-THIRD OF THE WORLD'S TOTAL.

NSW PRODUCED JUST 2 MILLION OUNCES.

Parliament House, Melbourne

Parliament House, Melbour...

Courtesy Parliament House

In the *Specification and Schedule of Quantities &c, Houses of Parliament,* by the Inspector of Works of 1885, the dome is listed as a separate cost of £54,500.4s.7d., but was never completed.

In the year 2000 estimates ran to a very unpopular and vote-threatening $4 billion.

In 1851 gold was discovered in Bathurst, NSW. Soon after it was also found in Victoria, and Melbourne exploded into a boom of development.

Two months after Melbourne's independence, Victoria had produced more gold than any other place on earth.

The city decided to show the world how grand, how well-heeled, and how civilised she really was, and so began the building of the great classical addresses of yesterday and today.

It was a building boom that would make today's developers green with envy. The extravagance was rivalled only by the pace at which buildings were erected. Melbourne changed from a 'canvas town' to a splendid capital on the proceeds of the goldfields. Up went the Houses of Parliament, the State Library, the General Post Office, the Royal Mint, the Treasury Building, the Melbourne Town Hall and St Paul's Cathedral.

The Grand Hotels were built (known later as the Menzies, the Windsor and the Scott Hotel), and the great theatres were opened.

Life was good, and money in great supply. Melburnians in the nineties drank more French champagne per head than the French. No wonder Melbourne was chosen to be the temporary capital of Australia in 1891 until Canberra was ready in 1927.

Melbourne's Government House is reputed to be the finest Vice-Regal address in all the British colonies. It features a ballroom of double ceiling height and an elaborate stencilled and gilded ceiling.

The Houses of Parliament building is the finest example of classical architecture in Australia. But it was never completed, and today remains without its dome, the finishing touch that will require another discovery of the magnitude of gold to fund its construction.

BOOM 1850s:	1860s:	1870s:	George's Emporium 1883
Buckley & Nunn 1852	Melbourne Town Hall 1867	Australia Club 1879	Princess Theatre 1887
Parliament House 1856–92	Royal Arcade 1869–70	Exhibition Buildings 1879–80	Stock Exchange 1888
State Library 1856	Royal Mint 1872		Rialto Building 1889
St Patrick's Cathedral 1858	Government House 1872	1880s:	Commercial Bank 1891
General Post Office 1859–67	Scots Church 1873	St Paul's Cathedral 1880	Block Arcade 1892
Treasury Building 1857	Supreme Court 1874	Windsor Hotel 1883	BUST 1893

THE VICTORIAN HOUSES OF PARLIAMENT WERE BUILT AS A TRIBUTE TO QUEEN VICTORIA. *Chandeliers, gilt paint and plasterwork, encaustic tiles, barrel-vaulted ceilings, ornate friezes and cornices, handsome wainscoting and elegant plaster panels suggest it was also built to show Sydney and the world just how good life was in Melbourne. As illustrated on these next pages, the building consists of the entrance vestibule, the Queen's Hall, the Legislative Assembly or Lower House, the Legislative Council or Upper House, and the Parliamentary Library, as well as smaller libraries, offices and function rooms.*

Legislative Council

The Queen's Hall

Parliamentary Library

melbourne's arms

Melbourne was the first of any Australian civic authority to adopt the kangaroo in its armorial bearings. Based on a seal engraved by Thomas Ham for the Melbourne Arms in 1843, the design consisted of a central shield containing in its four quarters a golden fleece, a whale, a bull and a ship, representing export trade in wool, oil and tallow. It was surrounded by a heraldic crest and featured a 'demi-kangaroo' — a bold departure from the traditionally British heraldic animals, the lion and unicorn.

This was the first step towards a truly unique and independent symbol for Victoria. Then in 1850, Dutch artist William Strutt arrived in Melbourne and began his prodigious and masterly body of illustrative work almost immediately. Very soon after his arrival, Strutt met John Pascoe Fawkner, who became a regular patron, recognising the Dutchman's immense talent, and also understanding the value of the artist in history, and in politics and statesmanship.

Their relationship was mutually beneficial, Fawkner finding his 'artist laureate', and Strutt, his patron.

Strutt experimented with heraldry, redesigning

#3

...ed with the permission of the Library Committee of the Parliament of Victoria from William Strutt's Victoria the Golden, Scenes, Sketches and Jottings from Nature 1850-1862

#2

the earlier Thomas Ham motif into the Melbourne Council Arms official seal, (#1) but his design was not adopted.

The use of the emu and kangaroo pair as armorial bearings follows in later sketches by William Strutt in 1850 (#2), and in a submission for the Arms for the Colony of Victoria (#3). This design contains the same quartered shield, flanked by a reclining emu and kangaroo pair, and features a lyrebird above the shield. Deemed too passive and elegant, this was also rejected. It was neither glorious nor pompous enough to reflect what the founding fathers saw as the go-ahead, energetic pride in progress that was the driving spirit of Victoria in the 1850s.

The 'demi-kangaroo' was ultimately retained in the final design for the armorial ensign for the Colony of Victoria of 1910 (#4), which gained two female figures, Peace and Prosperity (complete with olive branch and cornucopia) along with the Southern Cross, the Imperial Crown, and a wreath of the Colours Argent and Azure, all on a 'compartment' of grass. This design was further amended in 1973 to include the Victorian floral emblem — pink heath — and a revised St Edward's Crown in the kangaroo's grasp.

#4

Courtesy Department of Premier and Cabinet, Victorian State Government

MELB

Coote 2001

OPPORTUNITY | SANCT

A new design for Melb

William Strutt's 1850 s

the icons on the sh

tenets for Melbourn

HONI · SOIT · QUI · MAL · Y · PENSE

DIEU ET MON DROIT

DAME NELLIE MELBA 1861–1931
THE FIRST AUSTRALIAN SUPERSTAR,
A MELBOURNE GIRL.

You've gotta love a girl who is so marketing-savvy that she takes her city's name as her own. Like Kylie, she only needed one name. Like Kylie, she took the world by storm.

Born Helen Porter Mitchell, the daughter of Scottish immigrants, Melba grew up in Richmond, near Melbourne's city centre. Thanks to her father, who was a successful contractor and builder of the likes of Presbyterian Ladies' College, the Menzies Hotel and the Royal Exhibition Building, she was no stranger to privilege. Thanks to her undisputed talent, her naked ambition, and the invention of the gramophone, she became the world's first famous Australian woman. Her voice was heard and celebrated around the globe — she was our first touring superstar. In 1918, and without a drop of modesty, she claimed: "I put Australia on the map." And who can argue? Her role as ambassador for a remote city downunder to a distant international scene was worth a fortune in tourism awareness both to Melbourne and to Australia.

1961 STAMP
ISSUED TO
COMMEMORATE
MELBA'S
BIRTHDAY

Melba raised her daughter single-handed after her marriage failed, and was the highest paid performer of her time, remaining so for many years beyond her reign. Feisty and witty, she was at home in high society around the globe. Famous French chef Escoffier created and named a dessert for her — Pêche Melba — and she was entertained frequently by royalty. A coloratura soprano of unparalleled skill and talent, Melba performed at Covent Garden in London in 1888, and at La Scala in Milan and the Metropolitan Opera House in New York in 1893.

Nellie Melba was made a Dame of the British Empire in 1918, as reward for her war efforts in raising troop morale. She brought a strength of culture and achievement to Melbourne that it greatly needed. And she took Melbourne to the world. She was known as a "difficult" woman, which meant she was uncompromising — to her very great credit, and indeed, to that of Melbourne.

"THERE IS NO USE HAVING A PERFECT VOICE UNLESS YOU HAVE BRAINS, PERSONALITY, MAGNETISM, GREAT WILLPOWER, HEALTH, STRENGTH, AND DETERMINATION." MELBA

MELBA DIED IN A SYDNEY HOSPITAL IN 1931 FROM AN INFECTION ARISING FROM A FACELIFT OPERATION IN EUROPE

SIDNEY MYER 1878-1934

MERCHANT, VISIONARY, PHILANTHROPIST AND LOVER OF THE ART

'Myer's' is family. It's in the landscape. It's a cultural theme. It's always been there, and although it doesn't have the command of the marketplace it once had, it's still hard to imagine Melbourne without it. Its status as an icon is based one hundred per cent on its presence in our everyday lives, and that is based on its reputation for service, a direct reflection of the personal ethics of the man behind the business.

Proprietor Sidney Myer's own moral fortitude gave the company a personality like his own — trustworthy and accountable. One could not only buy anything at Myer, but also *return* anything to Myer, for any reason. A policy of such unquestioning respect for the customer's wishes did not result in abuse by the public, but rather created a unique relationship, jealously protected by both customer and store alike, building the kind of loyalty brands today can only dream of.

Sidney Myer's own character put such a strong stamp on the way the company did business with Melbourne that it has been rooted in Melbourne's history as more of a beneficent institution than a commercial enterprise. It is not insignificant that this entity, this icon, owes its success to its relationship with the women of this city.

Myer's dealings with them were couched in a common respect for community, family and decency, old-fashioned ideals that were the basis of Melbourne's culture and orientation. Sidney Myer's relationship with Melbourne's homemakers brought his name into the heart of every Melbourne family.

> "It is the responsibility of capital to provide work. If it fails to do this, it fails to justify itself."
> Sidney Myer

Simcha Myer Baevski, a Russian migrant from Kritchev, came to Melbourne in 1899 with nothing but the clothes he was wearing. He changed his name to Sidney Myer and went on to establish Australia's leading department store. As a tale of rags to riches opportunity, it's a classic. As a tale of migrant success, it is of outstanding value to his own family and to all new migrants. But what it really means to this city after 100 years of influence is so defining and fundamentally connected to the Melbourne psyche, that Myer became almost synonymous with the city's name.

Sidney Myer had a direct effect on the growing culture of the city, emotionally and physically reflecting and defining what Melbourne was all about. He nurtured, through his relationship with his customers, a spirit of fair play and honour that is fundamental to the Australian way.

After arriving at Port Melbourne, a 21-year-old Myer followed his brother Elcon to a new life, and joined him wrapping underwear at Slutzkin's factory in Flinders Lane, a mecca for drapers and tailors. When his English improved, he took to the streets as a door-to-door hawker of drapery and miscellaneous wares.

This time on the road taught him a lot, and set him dreaming. He was a strikingly handsome man, with fabulous eyes and marvellous manners, the ultimate combination for any salesman.

By 1900 the brothers had hawked their way to Bendigo, where they opened their first drapery store. Elcon's strict orthodox Jewish approach to business, and to issues like Saturday trading, clashed with Sidney's radical entrepreneurial spirit, and so Elcon returned to Flinders Lane and began his own business.

Sidney remained to begin his empire in Bendigo. This was Melba's time, Bendigo was thriving, and Myer's store thrived with it. Myer changed the face of retailing, removing the dividing obstacle of the counter, and replacing it with open tables strewn with goods to be touched and tested freely by customers. This was new, and completely different to the formality of over-the-counter requests. In effect it gave the consumer some control, some space in which to transact with the merchandise before buying.

Myer made exciting table displays that enticed customers and caused impulse purchasing. His displays were in fact the very basis of smart marketing. He knew that if goods are kept behind counters they remain unseen and unknown, and unsold.

Myer was a natural salesman, and his days of door-to-door were no doubt the time when he discovered through dealing direct with women on their doorsteps, that hands-on experience of the wares could create sales, and a genuine, personable manner could create repeat sales.

Myer wrote his own ads, displaying a marketing prowess ahead of his time. He understood the lure of a bargain, and of 'news-value' and excitement in advertising,

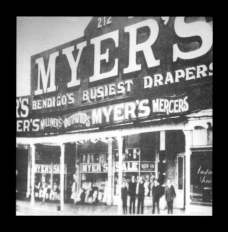

Above | Myer's first store at Bendigo

Below | Wright & Neil Drapery, site of the Myer Bourke Street Store

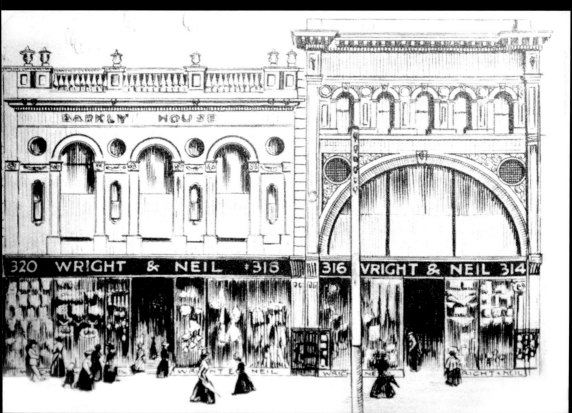

but he also understood the power of image in creating a lasting relationship with his customer. He understood the value of 'brand'.

He knew that the company name could infer a lot more than product. He advertised his store as a place 'where women and fashion gather', without any mention at all of product or price. He focussed on creating a sense of belonging to a special class for his patrons. He even addressed 'women emancipated' in attempts to connect with their hearts and passions. He wanted their loyalty, and their continued patronage. And so he was prepared to offer respect and service as well as his wares in order to get it. His business boomed, and by 1905 Myer completely dominated the Bendigo retail scene.

In 1911 Sidney Myer bought Wright & Neil drapery store in Bourke Street for £91,450 which from then on became Myer Bourke Street Store, and the very centre of the city, both physically and psychologically. The Bourke Street emporium was poised to become Melbourne's definitive retail icon.

He immediately raised the staff wages, and closed the doors for a massive stocktake, only to re-open them to stage Myer's first ever Myer Sale. Activity lasted a week. It was a launch to remember. Elcon now rejoined his brother, and a deputy was hired to run the Bendigo shops until their sale in 1914 for £50,000.

Sidney bought the freehold to the Bourke Street property in 1912, plus extra land in Post Office Place. In 1913 he bought a store in Flinders Street to temporarily house the growing business while a new emporium was built on the Bourke Street address. The eight-storey copy of a San Francisco emporium was opened in 1914, at a cost of £70,000.

Elcon handled the buying and imports, eventually becoming merchandising manager. Sidney set up local factories to supply his stores, and by 1917 had formed Myer Melbourne P/L, with himself and Neil (from the original drapery) as directors.

In the face of devastating depression in 1930 Myer invited 10,000 of the city's unemployed and homeless to share in his good fortune at a banquet he staged at the Royal Exhibition Building. He organised free tram transport, music, and gave a present to every child, and he and his staff waited on his guests personally.

The following year, in the depth of the

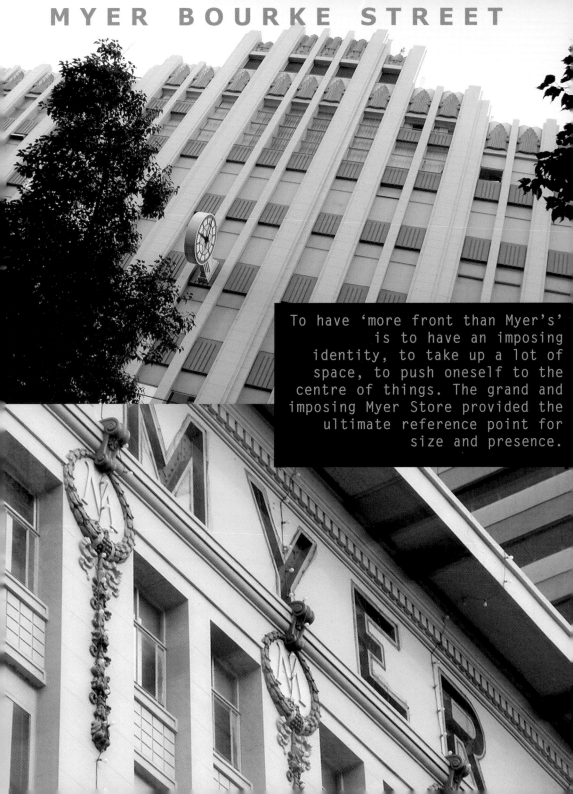

To have 'more front than Myer's' is to have an imposing identity, to take up a lot of space, to push oneself to the centre of things. The grand and imposing Myer Store provided the ultimate reference point for size and presence.

depression, Myer spent £250,000 on a renovation of the store deliberately to create employment and confidence in Melbourne's people. All staff suffered pay cuts so no one staff member would be retrenched. Myer's approach to management through hardship was model. He said: 'It is the responsibility of capital to provide work. If it fails to do this, it fails to justify itself.'

He urged other wealthy individuals and corporations to donate funds to government projects so people would have work and money for Christmas. He donated to the needy Melbourne University, Children's Hospital, Melbourne Symphony Orchestra, Shrine of Remembrance, Victorian Civil Ambulance Service, and gave his time to serve on the Melbourne Hospital Committee and the Committee of Victoria Centenary Council.

Sidney Myer died suddenly of a heart attack in 1934, at just 56 years of age. He left a fortune well over £1 million. One-tenth he directed to a charitable trust — The Sidney Myer Fund — for the philanthropic and educational needs of 'the community in which I made my fortune'. So far this fund has given today's equivalent of $100 million back to Melbourne.

A truly great institution, as a place to shop or a place to work, a place to meet, or as part of growing up, 'Myer's' as it was commonly known was the very model of a well-mannered, civil business. Parents sent their children to learn about the world of work in a part-time job at Myer. Mothers fed their babies in the shelter of the Ladies Lounge, where elderly ladies rested amidst the shopping bags and gloves of a big day out.

The generosity and community involvement that characterised Myer stores is no better displayed than through its Myer Christmas Windows. For over 50 years, the store has continued the tradition of creating intricate and delightful tableaux in its seven Bourke Street windows as a gift to the families and children of Melbourne since 1956.

Sidney Myer's legacy has been enormous, and marks a time when great businesses were truly community-spirited. His life and work is finally celebrated by a bronze statue tribute at the Sidney Myer Music Bowl, inscribed with the well-chosen words of his son Baillieu Myer: *Merchant, Visionary, Philanthropist and Lover of the Arts.*

Myer stands today on the site of two blocks of land in Melbourne's original land subdivision. These blocks were first purchased for £36 by John Batman in 1838. Batman, then living on the Yarra at Spencer Street — an area known as Batman's Hill — figured the town would blossom and grow more in his locale, so he sold the Bourke Street blocks in the same year, believing them to be worthless swamp. The buyer was Mr Elwynd Umphelby, a hotelier. Umphelby was also unhappy with the tendency for flooding in this low part of Bourke Street and decided to get rid of them as well. He promptly swapped them for a pregnant mare with a Mr Allan McDonald in the same year. From there the blocks were resold many times and used as cattleyards, public baths, a bookshop, and premises for a solicitor and a land agent. After the 1850s and the discovery of gold, Melbourne's population grew rapidly, and the grid district began to fill up. The two blocks were now among the most central and prime real estate in Melbourne. Better and better buildings came and went, until Barkly House was erected, which became the site for Anderson & Co, later Anderson & Brown, then Brown & Co, Brown & Osborne, Osborne & Wright, and finally Wright & Neil — a drapery — which was the business Sidney Myer bought for his Bourke Street store in 1911. The Myer Emporium was now positioned at Melbourne's retail centre.

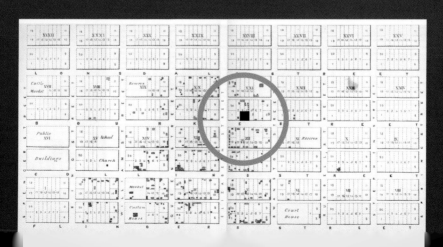

MACPHERSON ROBERTSON

If you drive across the Yarra River on the Mac Robertson Bridge and head down to the Domain, past the Mac Robertson Herbarium to where the Mac Robertson fountain plays at the base of the Shrine, you'll be very close to the Mac Robertson Girls High School. And, if you keep heading south, you'll eventually come to Mac Robertson Land in Antarctica.

Macpherson Robertson made his fortune from lollies. In early 1880, the ambitious 20-year-old began by making sweets in the bathroom of his Fitzroy family home. By 1888 he was running Mac Robertson's Steam Confectionery Works, and by 1925 Mac Robertson's Chocolates had a staff of 2500 employees.

Like Sidney Myer, Robertson made a brief trip to the USA where his imagination was fuelled by the great packaging ideas and inventive marketing he saw there. He came back to Melbourne and put it all into practice. He invited his employees to contribute ideas in exchange for bonuses. He pioneered sponsorships when he enlisted sporting clubs and cyclists to promote his all-new product, chewing gum. He painted his factory buildings white, dressed himself in a white suit, and his staff in white uniforms. Even the draught horses that pulled his white carts were white. His Fitzroy factory, known as the 'Great White City', was like a scene from Walt Disney's *Chitty-Chitty-Bang-Bang*, a sparkling sweets factory where clean, cheerful staff invented captions for 'conversation' sweets. And the staff were indeed cheerful, because Robertson was a champion of his workers, acting as their advocate in wages and conditions negotiations, and encouraging unionism, including the Women's Confectionery Worker's Union. He was a prominent figure in the street assemblies and marches for the Eight-Hour Day movement.

Mac Robertson wrested the control of the Australian confectionery industry away from the English importers who had dominated the market until then. He bought a controlling interest in the NSW 'Life Savers' (Australasia) Ltd brand and transferred its production from Sydney to Melbourne in 1926. He pioneered the manufacture of glucose in Australia, and brought the young nation its first ever chewing gum and fairy floss. Sherbets, marshmallows, toffees and sweets of all shapes and sizes were soon followed by chocolates from Old Gold to Cherry Ripe.

Like his contemporaries, Mac Robertson was a great philanthropist, donating £360,000 in gifts by 1933. He funded Antarctic expeditions, a herbarium at the Royal Botanic Gardens, and the first state Girls High School in Melbourne. His delicious business was left to his sons and grandsons, and was ultimately gobbled up, mostly by the Cadbury-Schweppes company.

With Mac Robertson's eponymous brand all but faded from memory, his connection is dissolving as fast as the words on a half-sucked lolly. But if you like a treasure hunt, you'll find some very concrete reminders of the legacy of Macpherson Robertson, Melbourne's very own, very real, 'Willy Wonka'.

c Robertson Land in Antarctica was named for Macpherson Robertson by Sir Douglas Mawson

ELBOURNE'S OWN WILLY WONKA

sanc

MELBOURNE

OPPORTUNITY | SANCTUARY | PASSION | BEAUTY

tuary

| liveability | trams | identity | royal botanic gardens | the shrine of remembrance | the port of melbourne | yarra yarra | private sanctuary | st kilda | the zoo | melbourne water | food |

world's most liveable city

The key to Melbourne's liveability lies in two major design elements. First, **the garden wedges.** Great chunks of green break into the metropolis bringing sanity, clean air, negative ions, shade, shelter, grace, autumn and spring. Second, and just as critical, is **the glorious width of the main city streets** — 99 feet wide. Robert Hoddle, Melbourne's surveyor, fought to keep them as wide as this in 1836, despite Governor Bourke's request to reduce them to 66 feet wide. The trade-off was a redefinition of the secondary streets as 'access lanes' designed to service each major street, and a reduction in their width to only 33 feet. Never meant to be used as streets, it distressed Hoddle that they were used exactly that way, almost immediately. Nevertheless, almost 200 years ago the lanes carry one-way traffic only and, Hoddle's grid manages the 21st century extremely well.

Melbourne's is the only surviving tram network in Australia, and the largest in the southern hemisphere. For 113 years, a rumble has combined with a ding and a cloud of grit to announce the arrival of a tram. 🚋 Both the first cable trams of 1885 and the electric trams of 1889 were seen as an exciting and glamorous ride. Despite having matured into a humble, familiar, reliable convenience, they can still be quite diverting. As the golden mean of architecture holds the secret to ideal human scale, so there exists the ideal rate of human progress on a tram. Never too fast or too slow, and a ride just long enough. 🚋 Once piloted by squads of either completely colourless or overly colourful staff, a tram was always much, much more than a conveyance. An intersection of lifestyles, a ride on a tram is always a great way to combine toffs and workers, yuppies and yobs. Examining each other side by side they sit, entertained until recently by a conductor spouting poetry or juggling coins for a captive audience. 🚋 When the world reinvented itself in the 1950s, a push arose for the removal of trams to make way for the car and a Modern Life. But a stubborn tramways union meant that trams were not going to be easily pushed aside. And Melbourne's wider than wide streets meant there was no great inconvenience to the car if they remained. So when other cities tore up their tracks, Melbourne trundled on into the 21st century. 🚋 Recently sold off by the Kennett government and now staffed by vending machines, trams are chasing a futuristic image. They are now defined by the lack of service and personality that belongs to all things privatised. 🚋 Much loved nonetheless, Melbourne's trams pump the blood of bustle around the city with incredible efficiency. Around 520 trams run on 240 km of track. Daily they knit a tracery of connections across Melbourne that rounds up the fringe dwellers, delivering them to and from the city's centre. Their continuing orbits keep the city at the heart of the action, and the action at the heart of the city.

TRAMS

Melbourne Tramway & Omnibus Co. Ltd.

NOTICE

To Gripmen and Conductors

Never take any chances of a Person, Carriage or Wagon getting out of the way. You
required to regard all persons coming at all in the way of the Car or Dummy as Infants
Deaf, or Blind, and when you know they are neither Infants, nor Deaf, nor Blind, you m
act on your part towards them as though they were, and it will be no excuse that
THOUGHT something. <u>What we demand is that you Stop, and take no chances.</u>

W G Sprigg Secret

c. 1

housewife | superstar

dame edna

"I'll never forget my roots in Melbourne...and I'm guessing they won't forget me either. Melbourne will always be close to my heart, like the Kleenex tucked inside my Hestia. Style, modesty, decorum: I learned it all in Melbourne."

identity

What's in a slogan? Identity is a big issue for people, products and places. Citizens are trained well as consumers and expect all products and most places to offer up a slogan to help identify themselves. This slogan, or positioning statement, is a shorthand definition designed to instantly explain identity, quality and character. Like any product or company, our states all have a tag line of their own. But when you're a young Australian state, it can be hard to identify your own most salient qualities. And so Queensland is no longer **The Sunshine State**, but now prefers **The Smart State**, despite a continuing preponderance of sunshine. South Australia is now sometimes **The Festival State**, and sometimes **The Wine State** but no longer **The State of the Arts**. Western Australia is no longer **The State of Excitement**, and is having a rest from both excitement and slogans at present. Tasmania, once **The Island State** (too obvious), has moved on to become **Your Natural State** (better) and NSW is not budging from **The Premier State**, right or wrong, ever.

Victoria – The Garden State — a most enviable tourism marketing description, was introduced in 1977 by then Premier Hamer, and endured for 17 years until it was replaced in 1994 by the Kennett government with **Victoria – On The Move**. This lasted for just six years before being moved along itself, and was then replaced for a time with merely **Victoria** until in October 2000 Premier Bracks installed a new tag line: **Victoria – The Place To Be.**

As one of the youngest cities in the world, still so close to our past and our future, it's hard to stand back far enough to see which factors are truly shaping our character and identity. A mild identity crisis is understandable. Time will best tell what is Victoria's most enduring and resonant quality. Meanwhile, it's hard to top the values of the **The Garden State**, a truly rare epithet in a world of spreading concrete. Melbourne's gardens — rare and valuable oxygen factories — not only make this city beautiful, but give us the ideal metaphor for Melbourne — fertile ground for ideas, deep-rooted passions, a solid body of established infrastructure, striving upward always, sustaining growth in all branches of endeavour, affording shelter and sanctuary for newcomers, and the peaceful good grace of a beautiful, healthy environment in which to enjoy it all.

L·IF·661 VICTORIA - GARDEN STATE

OMT·303 VICTORIA - ON THE MOVE

RIS·282 VICTORIA

QQN·STA VICTORIA - THE PLACE TO BE

Royal Botanic

Gardens Melbou

FRANCOIS COGNE BOTANICAL GARDENS 1863 LA

The pretty valley on the banks of the Yarra River that is home to today's Royal Botanic Gardens wasn't always so tranquil. From 1836 to 1841, this was the site of a government missionary school for Aborigines. In 1837 part of it was also used as Melbourne's first wholesale meat business and slaughterhouse.

By 1845 there was much debate in the blossoming young city about the selection of a site for a public garden, with FAWKNER lobbying hard for Batman's Hill to be the spot. But in 1846 it was settled, and this riverside valley was chosen as the home for what is today a majestic botanical gardens.

JOHN ARTHUR was appointed as head gardener, and in just a year he had created a fine showplace. When he died in 1849, local botanist DANIEL BRUCE took over his post, and a curator, JOHN DALLOCHY, was appointed to oversee the venture. Things flourished from there — part of the lagoon was excavated, and seeds were sent from exotic climes — Ceylon, Bombay, Madras, Singapore, Calcutta, and England. Even at this early stage there were 5000 exotic and 1000 indigenous plant varieties in Melbourne's impressive fledgling gardens.

MELBOURNE'S ROYAL BOTANIC GARDENS

"...ABSOLUTELY THE MOST BEAUTIFUL PLACE I HAVE EVER SE

- SIR ARTHUR CONAN DOYLE, CREATOR OF SHERLOCK HOLM

1920

ROYAL Botanic

BARON FERDINAND VON MUELL
(1825–1896)

In 1857 the site John Arthur and Daniel Bruce had tamed became the Melbourne Botanic Gardens, the third Botanic Gardens (behind Parramatta Gardens in NSW in 1800 and the Hobart Gardens of 1818 in Tasmania) since European colonisation.

Designed under the direction of German-born Ferdinand von Mueller, today's Royal Botanic Gardens owe their diversity and thoroughly scientific bent to his scholarly ideals. A migrant to South Australia in 1847, von Mueller was appointed the Government Botanist in 1853, a post he retained until his death. He immediately set off to join an expedition travelling 'across the top' from Darwin to Moreton Bay in order to amass a collection of tropical plants. For the next 16 years after his return in 1857, he created the Melbourne Botanic Gardens.

His dream was to create the 'complete works' of Australian plant life based on his expeditions in this living gardens collection, but the British botanical establishment at England's Kew Gardens 'commandeered' most of his best specimens and proceeded to incorporate them into a British publication, *Flora Australiensis*, by British botanist George Bentham.

The subsequent gardens director, W.R. Guilfoyle, turned von Mueller's strict and systematic presentation into a work of poetic rhythms. Guilfoyle abandoned the orderly scientific theme of von Mueller's gardens, transforming them with curving pathways, rolling lawns, follies, rotunda and waterways. He created surprises at the crest of every sweeping pathway. He led the visitor into lawned botanical rooms furnished with shrubberies and stones, or into great, green ballrooms of lawns bordered with gracious trees and trimmed in floral finery. Today every direction yields a vista of unexpected beauty. Guilfoyle painted with von Mueller's collection and created a masterpiece. The combination of the variety catalogued by von Mueller and the sheer artistry of Guilfoyle has blossomed into what is arguably the most expertly created gardens in the world. Dubbed 'Royal' in 1956, the garden by the Yarra became the Royal Botanic Gardens, Melbourne.

Gardens MELBOURNE

Beyond Botany

The Royal Botanic Gardens, Melbourne, houses the largest plant collection in Australia. It covers 38 hectares, and employs 200 staff. In an average year it hosts 1.98 million visitors, uses 1435 megalitres of water, and distributes 6–7 tonnes of fertiliser to the lawn areas alone. It is home to some 12,000 species of plantlife, plus some eels, possums, birds, bats and fish. Around 4000 new plants are planted each year, into a total plant collection of 52,000 plants in over two dozen different

garden collections, namely: the Oak Collection, Camellia Collection, Herb Garden, Fern Gully, Australian Rainforest Collection, Arid Garden, Species Rose Collection, California Garden, Water Conservation Garden, Cycad Collection, Lower Yarra River Habitat, Southern Chinese Collection, Grey Garden, Perennial Border, New Zealand Collection, New Caledonia Collection, Viburnum Collection and Canary Islands Collection. Features include the lagoon, the Ornamental Lake, the National Herbarium of Victoria, the Hot House, the Ian Potter Foundation Children's Garden, the Tea House, expansive lawns, summer movies en plein air, and sculptures by Louis Laumen, Michael Mezaros and Marc Clark.

Melbourne's green wedges are attributable to Governor La Trobe, who was instrumental in setting aside land for the Botanic Gardens, Royal Park, the Fitzroy Gardens, the Carlton Gardens and more. The discovery of gold saw the city develop so fast that the population grew from 29,000 in 1851 to 123,000 in 1854 — it more than quadrupled in three years — and there was a boom in building development in the inner city. It was a time of grandiose buildings and grandiose expenditure, so perhaps in that context, the generous indulgence of marking out huge tracts of land for glorious parks and gardens was not so hard to fathom. Considering the investment in time (16 years in the making for the Royal Botanic Gardens, Melbourne plus 150 years in the growing) and the value to tourism, these gardens are an asset that must be protected, and indeed championed as a leading attribute of Melbourne.

Royal Park

Treasury Gardens

Flagstaff Gardens

Carlton Gardens

Fitzroy Gardens

Royal Botanic Gardens Melbourne

St Kilda Botanic Gardens

The Kings Domain

St Vincent Gardens

The largest sculpture commission in Melbourne's history

THE SHRINE OF REMEMBRANCE

BUILT FROM 1928 TO 1934

DURING THE YEARS OF THE GREAT DEPRESSION

THE SHRINE OF REMEMBRANCE

The Shrine of Remembrance was built to honour those who served and died in WWI, 1914–1918. The building is the result of a public design competition among local Melbourne artists and architects. From 83 submissions the final design selected, which we see today, is the creation of two returned soldiers and architects, Peter Hudson and James Wardrop.

Designed in the style of a Greek mausoleum — specifically the memorial to King Mausolos of Caria in Southern Greece around 300 BC — it is a most impressive and dramatic structure. Its exterior is imposing and majestic. Its interior is designed to allow a narrow beam of light to shine like a laser onto a central plaque of remembrance within. Beneath this lies the crypt, a place to house records of names of soldiers, battalions, regiments and the memorabilia of war.

This was the largest ever sculpture commission in Melbourne's history at the time. The sculptures and reliefs were designed by English immigrant Paul Montford, who had made Melbourne his home. Throughout the 1920s and 30s his work was highly regarded and many of his pieces grace Melbourne's parks and gardens. The exquisite carved friezes that line the interior chamber are the work of a young Lyndon Dadswell, then just 22 years old. They depict the various activities of servicemen and women in a graceful art deco relief.

Funding such a huge project on the verge of the Great Depression presented a problem. An appeal was launched to raise funds to build the monument in 1928, very lean times for most Australians. Yet millions of ordinary families contributed the necessary £250,000 for work to begin. In fact the funds to build the buttress sculptures were raised almost entirely by children's school groups, in pennies and small donations, a fact commemorated by the sculptor in the child figure that steadies the lions in each buttress group. Sidney Myer donated £5000 to the effort in 1932. Work was carried out over six years and completed in 1934.

THE SHRINE STANDS APART FROM US, YET REMAINS VISIBLE FROM ALL DIRECTIONS, TO REMIND US OF OUR SMALL BUT SIGNIFICANT PLACE IN HISTORY. GLOWERING LIKE A CRUSTY OLD GRANDFATHER IT LOOKS DOWN FROM YESTERDAY DEMANDING THAT WE REMEMBER, AND THEN GET ON WITH IT.

ASUKA

f melbourne

It doesn't really matter what kind of boat you arrived in, Melbourne is made of boat people. Convicts and settlers from the tall ships of England, Greeks and Italians on the liners from Europe, Asian refugees on a voyage to freedom. The resulting mix of people find themselves all in the same boat. It's the world's best ever second chance, and one that demands appreciation. The history lesson of Melbourne is just this: here, this time, we all get a chance to get it right. Let's not forget our origins and need a third chance. It's highly unlikely there'll be one.

the port of melbourne

After the European settlement of Melbourne in 1835, shipping activity centred around the place on the Yarra River known as The Falls, where the port was established at the widest part of the river. But getting there from the river mouth at Hobson's Bay could prove difficult.

'The Yarra river was a nuisance...The stretch of river was eight miles long and winding and shallow. It could take hours for a ship to avoid the sandbars and reach Melbourne...' [1]

The river route was time-consuming and inconvenient. Eight miles of sailing upstream against the flow of the Yarra meant many passengers chose to disembark at Sandridge Beach (today's Port Melbourne). Here, an enterprising new arrival named Wilbraham Liardet built a tea-tree jetty for just this purpose (below).

Liardet had arrived in Melbourne in 1839,

and, unable to buy a lift from vessel to beach, bought his own boat and began a business , ferrying passengers from ship to shore and then transporting them or their luggage by road from the beach to Melbourne Town.

He built his jetty soon afterward, began a mail-run and opened the Pier Hotel on the corner of Bay and Beach streets in 1840. When Liardet arrived in Melbourne the

APPROACH TO MELBOURNE, 1844
La Trobe Library Collection

population was 4000. Government Surveyor Robert Hoddle had included some plans for the beach in his work in 1839, but these were not implemented until some 15 years later. And so the beach shaped itself in a more organic fashion, based around necessity and opportunity.

Liardet's business blossomed. He had grand hopes to name the beach Brighton, but by this stage it was popularly known as Liardet's Beach, or Sandridge.

Meanwhile, the Yarra River port at The Falls had become the site of the Customs House, warehouses, markets and hotels. But after 12 years or so, and despite dredging and the removal of the rocks of The Falls themselves, the limitations of the shallow river port

LIARDET'S PIER: 'THE FIRST LANDING PLACE AT SANDRIDGE 1840' *from Victoria Today: A Review 1851-1901, La Trobe Library Collection*

[1] FROM *A HISTORY OF PORT MELBOURNE* by NANCY U'REN & NOEL TURNBULL

became too restrictive, and Melbourne sought a place to create a more substantial shipping facility. The government favoured Williamstown for this purpose, and spent a great deal of money developing the town and the port area in the 1850s. Meanwhile, a privately developed port at Sandridge was progressing, and was eventually chosen above Williamstown as Melbourne's preferred port.

After all, it was closer to the city, and had its own rail line — the first in the entire country — which opened in 1854.

Princes Pier was constructed from 1912 to 1915, and worked as a busy trade port through to the 1930s, providing the launching place for many new migrants up until 1969.

Station Pier was built between 1922 and 1930 and is the largest timber wharf structure in Australia. It received migrant ships in the 1950s and 60s and serviced overseas shipping requirements from the 30s until the 70s, when air freight and container shipping changed the face and nature of port activity forever.

Station Pier is permanent home to the Devilcat ferry, and to the Spirit of Tasmania, which crosses Bass Strait to Tasmania twice weekly. On 27 February 2001, Station Pier enjoyed its first full house in 27 years, with three international cruise ships berthed alongside the Tasmanian Devilcat ferry. Since then all four berths have been regularly filled with ferries and luxury liners.

Melburnians love to flock to Station Pier and see the ships come in. The smell of oil and rust and greasy salt transports us to wondrous worlds apart. For many it has been the end of the line or the start of the new world. The very first memories of Melbourne are here for so many immigrants, for soldiers, for sailors. Wet, desperate, frantic farewells continue to take place as big ships pull away from the dock. And despite the end of the gracious good times for steamship travel, we are now seeing a new love affair with the luxury liner, — as the ship contests the long-held supremacy of the aeroplane for luxury travel. And as history would have it, just as Melbourne is discovering its waterfront as the ideal address for 21st century apartment living.

'STUDY FOR THE YARRA RIVER' 1991 BY WENDY FOARD

Once fresh water all the way down to The Falls, the Yarra River was always the source of life in the undisturbed scrub by Port Phillip Bay. So, too, it became the centre of enterprise in the new, colonial Melbourne after 1835. But almost immediately the booming city drew the focus away from the Yarra. The river was soon second best to new and exciting road and rail networks. Relegated to being crossed over, drawn from and dumped into for nearly a century, the last thing anyone wanted to do was look at the Yarra. It laboured ingloriously as the central nervous system of shipping at one end, and provided small time leisure boating at the other. But the central city river expanse was largely ignored and much maligned for decades. It took until the 1990s for the river's renaissance as the jewelled necklace of Melbourne. A concerted effort to clean up the river and curb pollution, combined with a new appraisal of the river real estate, began a decade of change. First recast as the ideal tourist destination, cafés, hotels and galleries began to appear. Southgate, Crown Casino, Melbourne Exhibition Centre, and Pier 35 begin the list of new additions to the south bank. Next, defined as the ideal residential address for the 21st century, the notion of a river view from a city apartment revalued the Yarra as prime real estate. What once languished unloved and uncherished became highly prized. The back-door business of Melbourne is being systematically removed to accommodate front-of-house luxury. Wharfs and docks are being transformed into glittering office spires or towers filled with 'lifestyle solutions'. Threaded with brighter and brighter beads, the necklace is fast becoming a dazzling cord as Melbourne and time have once again flipped the Yarra's fortunes upside down.

Early settlers mistook the generic Aboriginal words *Yarra Yarra,* meaning 'flowing-flowing', for the name of Melbourne's river. In fact its Aboriginal name is '*Birr-arrung*', which describes 'water coursing through mist and umbrageousness'... flowing under the deep and dappled shade of leafy trees. Before white men disturbed the nirvana of Port Phillip Bay, the Yarra boasted clear waters and abundant fish:

'The waters were bright and sparkling, and wooed by the fragrant acacias, shaking their golden blossom curls...'

'The Yarra also swarmed with a sort of blackfish, bream, flounder and herring'

'The porpoises not only used to venture out of the bay into the saltwater river, but were sometimes rash enough to indulge in an aquatic stroll as far as Richmond.'

These words written by local historian EDMUND FINN went on to lament the state of what 50 short years of colonial habitation had done to this idyll by **1888**: '...how different in aspect and aroma from the Yarra of today — a foetid festering sewer, befouled midst the horrors of woolwashing, fell-mongering, bone-crushing and other unmentionable abominations!'

Since white settlement in the early 1830s, and since Finn's 1880s, millers, dyers, breweries, slaughterhouses, papermills, fabric mills, and every other conceivable manufacturer have used and abused our stubborn, mysterious Yarra. No wonder she flows upside down.

Extracts from *The Chronicles of Early Melbourne 1835 to 1852: Historical, Anecdotal and Personal by Garryowen* by Edmund Finn, Heritage Publications, Melbourne, 1976.

Yarra Yarra

The Sandridge Rail Bridge was Australia's first rail bridge, built for Australia's first rail line. Trains from the city Terminus first ran to Port Melbourne on this line in 1854. Closed in 1987, it is destined to become a pedestrian walkover from Flinders Street to the recently reinvented river front on the south bank.

WESTGATE BRIDGE 1978

BOLTE BRIDGE 2000

CHARLES GRIMES BR. 2000

SPENCER ST BR. 1930

KINGS BRIDGE 1961

QUEENS BRIDGE 1889

SANDRIDGE RAIL BR. 1854

FOOTBRIDGE

PRINCES BRIDGE 1853–88

SWAN ST BRIDGE 1952

MORELL BRIDGE 1899

HODDLE ST BRIDGE 1938

SOUTH YARRA RAIL BRIDGE

CHURCH ST BRIDGE 1924

MAC ROBERTSON BRIDGE 1943

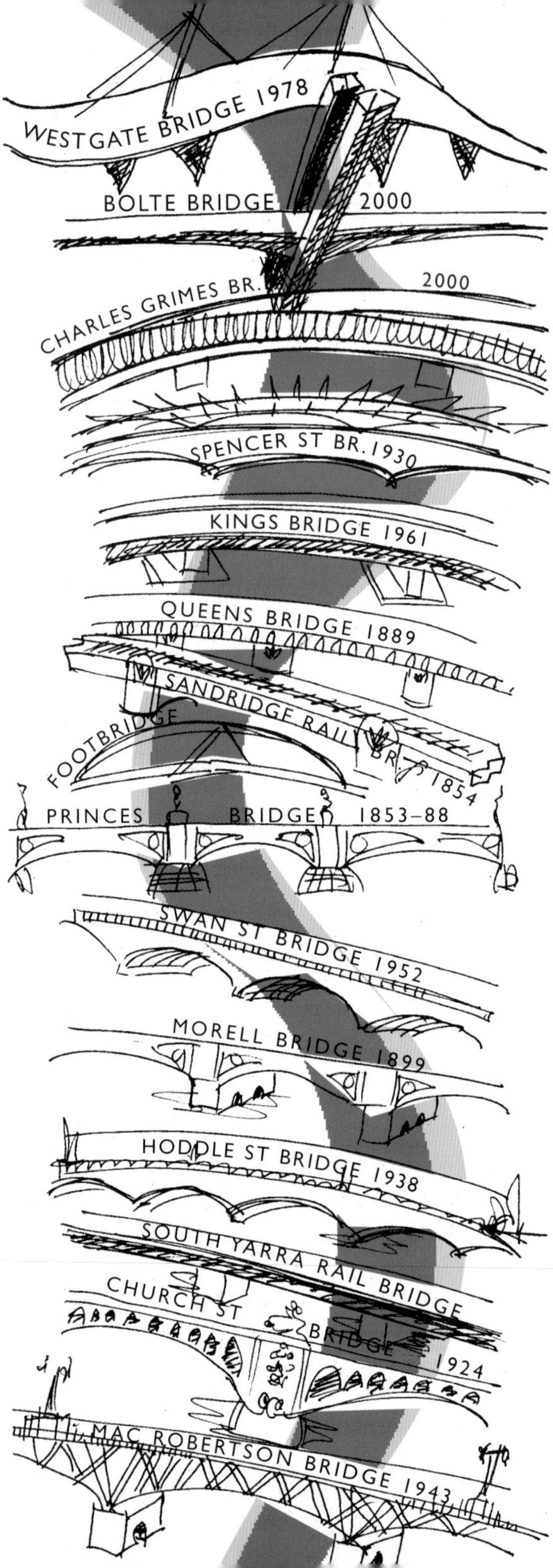

The first punt to operate river crossings was *The Melbourne*, named after the British PM, and operated by William Watts in 1838.

Then came the ferries, the first of these a father and daughter enterprise named *The Charon*.

But daily traffic soon demanded a bridge, so in 1840 the Melbourne Bridge Company was formed.

Governor La Trobe's plan was to cross at Elizabeth Street, but the Melbourne Bridge Company favoured Swanston Street, where it was both shallower and less muddy.

Commonsense prevailed, and Princes Bridge was built as a one-arch span in 1853, and later widened to three arches in 1888.

where the river flows upside dow

PRIVATE SANCTUARY
the Savage club

Originally built as a private home in 1884, 12–16 Bank Place appears a sedate and unprepossessing stone building. But there's a lot more to this quiet façade, because in 1923 it was sold to the Savage Club, and remains the home of this exclusive club today.

The Savage Club began in England in 1857, named after English poet Richard Savage. Members included writers, poets and artists — the leading lights of their day like W. M. Thackeray, Charles Dickens, and even Mark Twain when visiting London. The aim of the Club was 'to promote social intercourse', and it encouraged the patronage of 'music, dramatic, artistic, scientific and literary professions, and sculptors and ordained clergymen of all denominations...'. The menu cards and posters drawn for the club by its own caricaturists show how well the members celebrated '..."humorists of pen and pencil", who made "thought provoking drawings and wrote mirth provoking songs, ... especially one about a military bandsman who blew out his viscera through the trombone"...'

The fraternity found its way to Melbourne amongst new colonials, and the Melbourne Savage Club was founded in 1894. The 'Savage' theme is expressed through representations of native lifestyle and bohemian spirit, brought to life in a collection of exotic artefacts, and in the renderings of the club's own menus and invitations. While revering the essence of bohemian freedoms, these often displayed the patronising racism of the time and a great ignorance of the races of the world that were the symbol of an exotic nineteenth century ideal.

The Melbourne Savage Club's interior decor conjures up a Victorian version of Walt Disney's Frontierland. Here a select group of men escape to refined conversation amidst raw decorations, to ingest fine food and wine in a setting of affected barbarism. Bohemian themes course through this dark brown, primal decor as background to more civilised pursuits like music, art, and literary discourse. The walls of the three-storey Club are clad in dark wood wainscoting, and hung with paintings and antiquities, in a rare and eccentric collection of both primitive art and art depicting primitives. Bare-chested native 'savages' drawn in colonial times and framed in colonial gilt adorn the walls, along with spears and shields, while a totem pole rises up the core of the stairwell.

Downstairs in the vast main dining hall, a pair of gigantic hearths yawn at each end of the room, while over the mantle are displayed native armoury and taxidermy aplenty. Upstairs a small bar is decorated with the masculine graphics of framed press cartoons from early copies of the likes of *Punch* and *The Bulletin*, crammed tight among the clutter of manly trophies and souvenirs.

The Savage Club is a marvellous, musky, mannish haven, boasting members from S.T.Gill to Arthur Streeton and Frederick McCubbin to Robert Menzies. Quiet, quirky, raucous, snoring and undisturbed for nearly 80 years, it is a shrine to the gloriously peculiar, and deliriously eccentric. To most Melburnians it remains a great secret. But to its elite membership it offers a vivid hallucination of and transportation to another world and another time.

THE MELBOURNE SAVAGE CLUB

EX LIBRIS

"A pleasant land, ...a land over which
hangs an endless fog, occasioned by much
tobacco; a land of chambers, billiard-
rooms, supper-rooms, oysters; a land of
song; a land where soda-water flows freely
in the morning; a land of tin dish-covers
from taverns, and frothing porter; a land
of lotus-eating (with lots of cayenne
pepper);... a land where men call each
other by their Christian names, where
most are poor, where almost all are
young, and where if a few oldsters do
enter, it is because they have preserved
more carefully and tenderly than other
folks their youthful spirits."

*Bohemia as described by
London 'Savage',
William Makepeace Thackeray*

Native Dignity

St Kilda

Home of Australia's very first Luna Park, St Kilda is where Melbourne keeps its sense of humour. Like Toyland on acid, it is whacky, novel, was once quite bohemian and is always slightly nuts. It is a theme park of a suburb, home to night clubs and the notorious Melbourne red-light district. Plenty of palm trees and plaster façades continue a tradition of holiday distractions and dreamlike unreality. Originally it was named Euro-Yroke after the Aboriginal word for the red sandstone found there. The village was renamed St Kilda during an exclusive beach picnic around 1841 attended by Superintendent (later Governor) La Trobe and party. The original Mr J. B. Were was also present, part-owner of the yacht *Lady of St Kilda* which was moored just off the beach. Guests made trips from picnic to yacht throughout the day, and when talk turned to the forthcoming Government land sale of the area, La Trobe was asked what name they should give the place. He looked up from his champagne, spied the *Lady of St Kilda* and named the town after it then and there. In 1906, St Kilda was acknowledged as a significant pleasure resort, and two hectares of its area were redesigned into a reserve devoted to the 'Recreation, Convenience and Amusement of the People'. Here, a pleasure palace called Dreamland offered hours of fun for just three shillings and sixpence, and later in 1912 the first Luna Park in the country was opened, cementing St Kilda's identity as the funny bone of Melbourne.

St Kilda

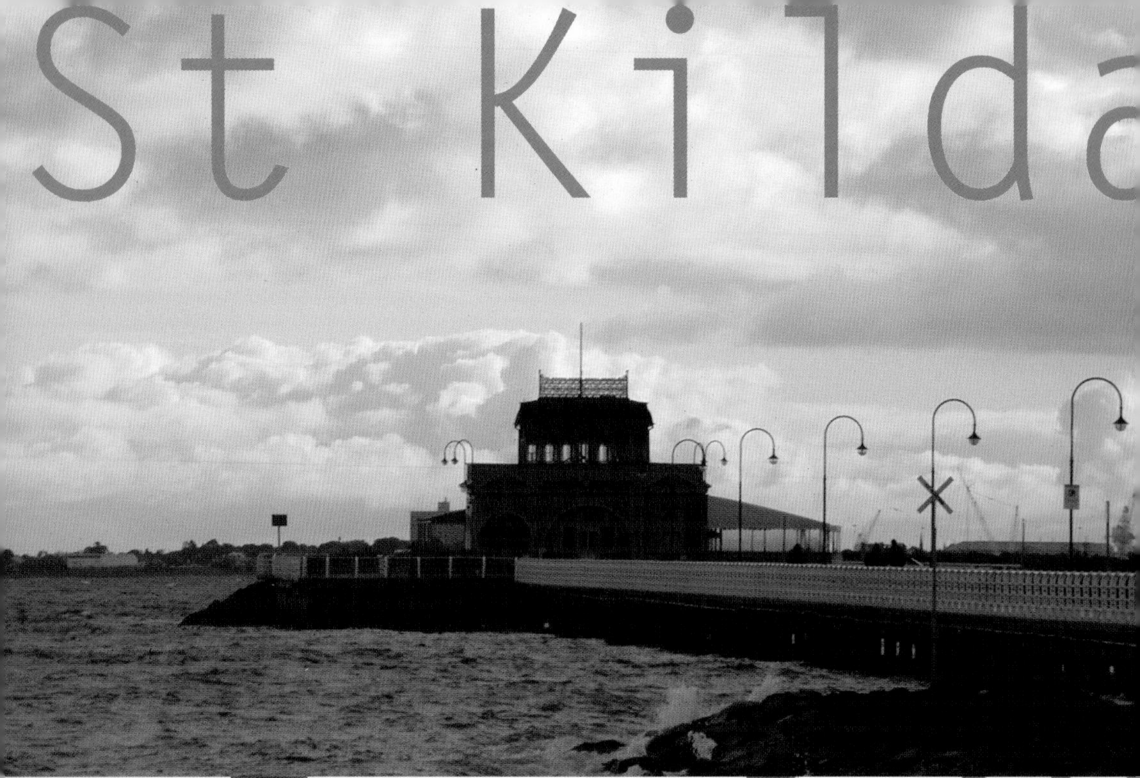

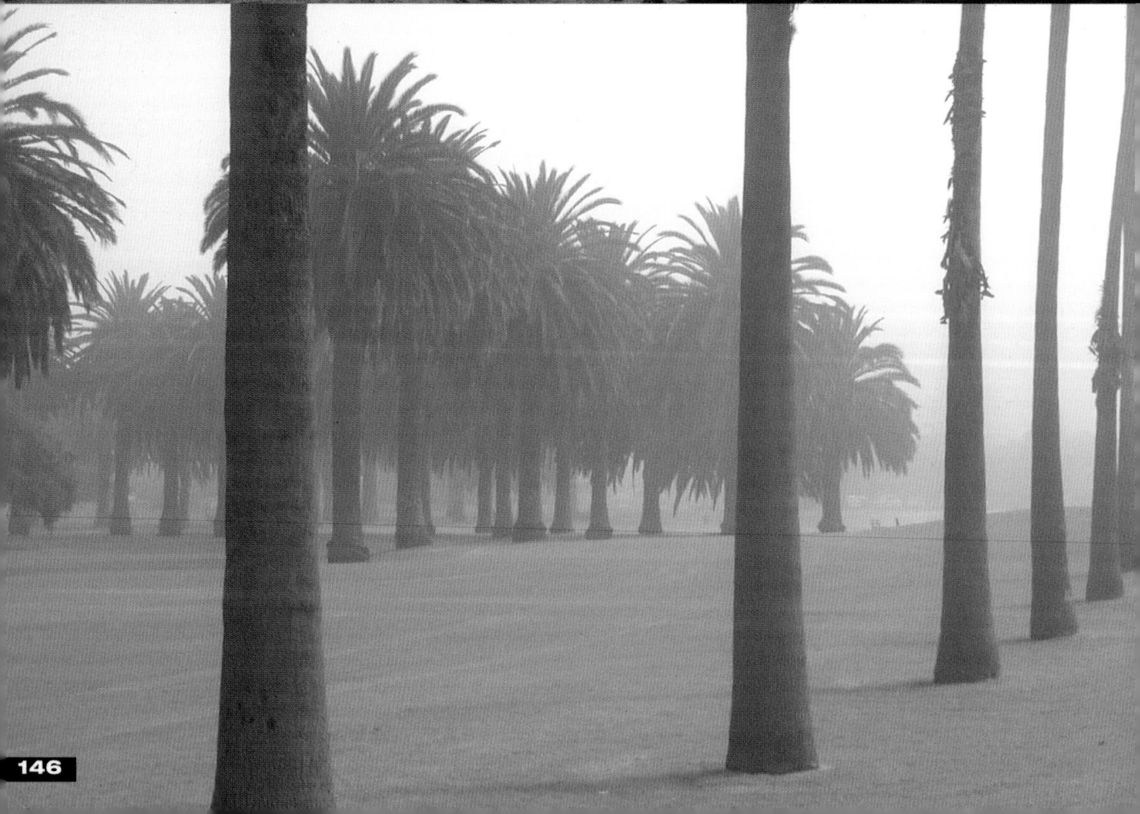

In 1857, the second railway in the colony was built from Melbourne to the St Kilda Terminus.
In 1906, two hectares of carnival pleasure palace called Dreamland offered nine hours of fun for 3s 6d.
In 1912, Luna Park was opened, designed by Eslick and Corbeille, creators of New York's Coney Island.

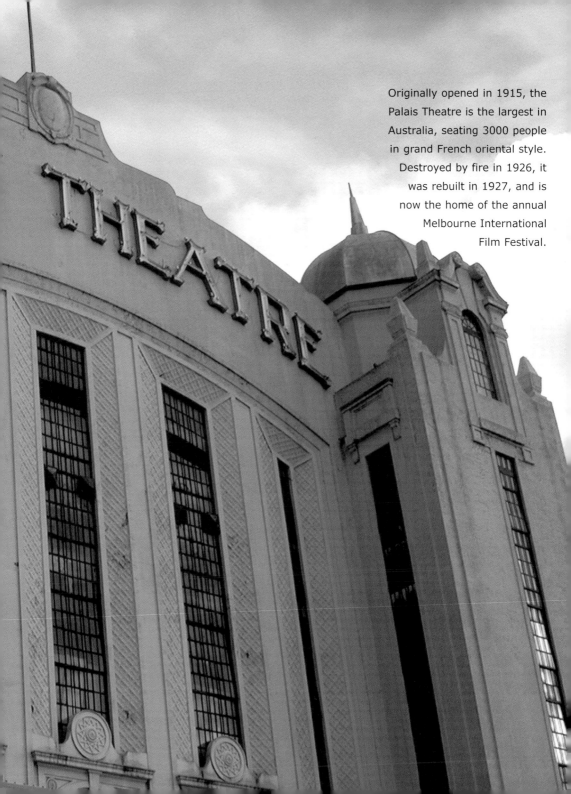

Originally opened in 1915, the Palais Theatre is the largest in Australia, seating 3000 people in grand French oriental style. Destroyed by fire in 1926, it was rebuilt in 1927, and is now the home of the annual Melbourne International Film Festival.

The oldest Zoo in Australia

Although it's the animals that attract us to the Zoo as children, somehow it's not the animals that linger in the memory. A lifetime later, it's the Zoo itself that calls us back. It has a personality like no other place.

Although Melbourne Zoo is one of the most modern and forward-thinking zoos in the world, parts of the park are now heritage-listed treasures of Melbourne's past, including the main drive with its glorious date palms planted in the 1860s, the giraffe enclosure and even the intricate brick fence that borders the zoo's perimeter. Historic cages, turnstile gates and weighing machines seem as exotically different today as the animals themselves.

There's a marvellous air of the surreal about the Zoo: some kind of wondrous mood of suspended animation. The graceful botanic entry leads us back to the scene of picnics and ungainly elephant rides. Fake rock landscapes and unlikely animal enclosures remind us always of the abstract unreality of the zoo concept, the constructed nature of it all. Off the main drive, exciting new concepts in habitat presentation contrast the old, highlighting just how far we've come in our understanding of the care of animals. A rich and textured environment, the Melbourne Zoo is the original, the supreme theme park, to be treasured as much for its remarkable artefacts and structures as for its inhabitants.

The first Zoological Society of Melbourne established itself on the banks of the Yarra River opposite the Botanic Gardens in 1857. It boasted a small collection of Australian native animals accented with a few monkeys, and for its first four years was overseen by Botanical Gardens director Ferdinand von Mueller.

After its move in 1862 to its present site at Royal Park, The Zoo Society became known as the Acclimatisation Society of Victoria, the title acknowledging its role in supplying the young colony with breeding stock, pets (and pests), just like those back in England. It was a practical place where newly arrived animals adjusted to the antipodean conditions before moving on to farms or freedom. Then, around 1870, under the guidance of Albert le Soeuf, the Society began to acquire more and more exotic animals – starting with lions, tigers and bears.

Permanent brick display enclosures were constructed from the 1890s onward. In 1928 the formal gardens and botanical beds at Royal Park were laid out. Melbourne's celebrated landscape and garden designer Edna Walling was invited to submit for the project and created a series of designs for the Zoo gardens in that same year, but her designs were never realised. The institution was eventually renamed the Zoological Board of Victoria in 1937, finally dropping the 'acclimatisation' reference completely.

Today the two remaining original 19th century brick cages stand as museum pieces only, no longer deemed fit to confine large animals. Eighty years of elephant rides begun in 1883 ceased forever in 1962, as the circus and side-show nature of the early years of the Zoo has been steadily transformed into a more relaxed, natural habitat.

The Melbourne Zoo is continually adapting to changes in the standards of habitat and presentation. Beyond the formality of the historic zone along the main drive, new naturalistic habitats are constantly being created for the improved comfort of the animal inhabitants.

Most of the modern building work was done in the 20 years since 1960, under the direction of Alfred Dunbavin Butcher, including the Great Flight Aviary (longest walk-through aviary in the world), the Lion Park (first walk-over big cat enclosure in the world), the Reptile House, the Arboreal Primate Walkway, and the Butterfly House. More recently, open and natural habitats have transformed the Zoo with relaxed and lifelike rainforest settings specifically designed for gorillas, hippos, mandrills and tigers. An insect house has extended the Butterfly House, and by 2003 the elephants will enjoy an expansive new trail habitat.

The Zoo became the 'Royal' Melbourne Zoo in 1977, and today the Zoological Parks and Gardens Board also manages Healesville Sanctuary and Victoria's Open Range Zoo at Werribee.

THOMS
1,068,000

CARDIN
287,000

UPPER YAR
200,000

SUGARLO
96,000

SILVA
40,000

YAN YE
30,000

GREENVA
27,000

MAROONDA
22,000

O'SHANNAS
3000

APPROX. 1,773,0
MEGALITR
TOTA
CAPACI

MELBOURNE USES 50,000 ML O
WATER A YEAR. THAT'S 330,00
OLYMPIC POOL'S FUL

melbourne water
THE WORLD'S BEST DRINKING WATER

Melbourne is one of only six cities in the world with a water resource this good. (Okay, that's Seattle, Portland, San Francisco, Vancouver and Victoria, Canada.) Pure water that flows from untouched forest. Thanks to the vision of the 1853 Melbourne Board of Commissioners of Sewers and Water Supply, we drink the world's sweetest drop. In 1857, Yan Yean reservoir was built as the first of a system of 14 reservoirs covering over 140,000 hectares of forest land. This is the natural factory that captures Melbourne's water supply. A basin of Mountain Ash covered hills that funnel rainwater down into a pristine water storage dam. Catchments closed to the public for over 100 years means no contaminants. Indigenous eucalypts of immense age mean old trees that use much less water than young trees, providing far more runoff for catchment. Water remains in these catchments for over five years to allow for natural purification before draining through to the city supply system, your tap, and your glass. Enormous human and natural endeavour has created this invaluable resource over hundreds of years. It will take more of the same to protect it into the future. Lately, logging has been permitted in parts of the Thomson and Yarra catchments. Although the activity is small, it brings the threat of contamination to water from humans and soil disturbance, increased costs to treat water discolouration and inevitably less water catchment as young, thirstier trees replace their ancestors. Right now, however, Melbourne's water is just about the best in the world. So drink up.

food

food

After decades of home-country poverty, military mess tents, sea-going swill, gruel and stew, potato famines, scurvy and weevils in the flour...antipodean tummies gradually relaxed into new decades of the predictablility of plenty — the sweet security of meat and two veg. It's not surprising the focus was on tummies, not tongues. But not for long, thanks to the steady stream of mostly european migrants, who despite the initial ridicule of the contents of their school lunchboxes, eventually had Melbourne beginning to taste things previously only ever described as 'bait'.

Great food is essential in Melbourne. Like dressing well, Melburnians are hard-wired to eat well. It's never been about quantity or showbiz. It was always about real food, made from real lives.

Melbourne's European and Asian migrants transformed the bland Anglo-Saxon table into a feast of flavours, and taught us how to eat. Real food comes from centuries of cultural tradition, and yet this remarkably young city — an infant in the scheme of things — has the gift of all the time and knowledge of traditional kitchens, delivered fresh to a courageous table. Since the gold-diggers of the 1850s brought real coffee to Little Bourke Street and bok choy to Ballarat, Melbourne has gradually grown into enjoying tentacled seafood, sticky-sweet cakes, endless noodles and variegated vegies.

Melbourne's migrant settlers have brought the city the world's best recipe for lifestyle, and the secret is authenticity. It's the Life that makes the food — the life of the fisherman, the gardener, the grandmother, the daughters.

Real food begins at home. Real flavour comes from families, and from the seasons. A limited budget and a reliance on homegrown and self-caught produce is a recipe for endless creativity. In homeland villages, the absence of alternatives led Europeans and Asians to centuries of bottling, pickling, marinading, curing, stuffing — employed to avoid monotony at the table. Twenty ways to serve a squid, and 50 different shapes of pasta are inventions that result from this connectedness with the garden and sea.

Without this link to the source and seasons of food, the modern style can become a flashy fashion parade of exotica for its own sake, or worse — international menus offering too much too often. Mangoes out of season, and prices out of this world. Not on Melbourne's table, which is a place of rich connection, and endless variations on a theme.

Melbourne was pivotal in the invention of the new Australian cuisine, now the model for dedicated foodies not only in Australia, but all over the world. Always creative, but always focused on quality, Melbourne food is about flavour, not fads. The combination of the European and Asian traditions of time-consuming and explorative approaches to recipes combined with the high quality of produce Melbourne offers has created a rich freedom in the kitchen.

Confident and strengthened by these blended origins, Melbourne's table offers a truly multicultural menu. Courageous and conservative at the same time, Melbourne's food respects its roots, while exploring new ways. Brilliant food is flopped onto plain white plates with an expectation of perfection, a mood of true friendship, and an appreciation of quality. None of the glitz, but all of the greatness. Anything goes, as long as it's the best there is.

pas

OPPORTUNITY | SANCTUARY | PASSION | BEAUTY

sion

66 Melbourne is where ideas are generated. The film industry began in Melbourne but Sydney built the studios. The authors are in Melbourne, but Sydney had the publishers. The painters were in Melbourne, but the galleries were built in Sydney. I don't know if it's something in the water or the weather...but Melbourne was and remains our intellectual capital. **99**

phillip adams

PHILOSOPHER, BROADCASTER, WRITER, THINKER, HUMORIST AO

The gloves are finally off between Melbourne and Sydney. No more apologies. Melburnians call Sydney brash, cheap, shallow and chintzy. Sydney-siders say Melbourne is dull, dull, dull.

At the bottom of it all is sibling rivalry. Like all good blues, it is best dealt with on the footy field or even better, in the language: Melbourne is the brains, Sydney the brawn. If Sydney is International, Melbourne is Cosmopolitan. Sydney is new money, Melbourne is old money. Sydney is entrepreneurial, Melbourne is well-connected. Sydney is flashy, Melbourne is quality. Sydney is convict stock, Melbourne is landed gentry. And therein lies the key: the fundamental rift is one of class and origin.

own dignified time, and it refuses to be dazzled by shiny objects like Sydney.

Melbourne character is a kind of hybrid of the wowser/radical. It's establishment, but bolshy. It's cultured but political. Like Germaine Greer, it has class and attitude. Intelligence and passion. The wit of Barry Humphries, the soul of Michael Leunig. The only Sydney thing we wish we had is our Phillip Adams back.

In the 1980s Prime Minister Bob Hawke tried to introduce Japanese-language street signs to Melbourne. In the 1990s, Premier Kennett swamped Melbourne's Moomba by taking over Adelaide's Grand Prix and scheduling the latter on the very same Moomba weekend.

melbourne vs sydney

From a Melbourne perspective, Sydney will always be inferior. Melbourne's arts, culture, food, fashion, and overall style have always been better. Sydney is basically outclassed at every turn.

The great Phillip Adams once said that Sydney is expert at commercialising anything originated in Melbourne. Like David Williamson, the Olympics, and Food. And now they've got Phillip himself. We think, talk, invent ideas in Melbourne, and Sydney takes them on. Exploits them. Implements them. Like the writer and the showman. As an ideas factory, Melbourne's a runaway success.

Melbourne's weather makes it a more intellectual city — more indoorsy and well-read. Melbourne's history gives it a less desperate beginning. Melbourne's measured pace takes its

It's a common mistake, not being able to see Melbourne's unique character for the trees. The taste and flavour of Melbourne is like no other city in the world. It's a city for great thoughts and deep passions. Renowned for its restaurants, its artists, its writers and thinkers, Melbourne grows totally unique fruit.

Cities are the authentic and ultimate theme parks, best when they are as original as possible. Only then do they offer the real diversion of a unique experience. Local colour, local language and local eccentricity should be protected from any push towards homogeneity.

So let's hope the siblings keep on wrestling – Brains and Brawn – forever resisting uniformity. After all, the writer and the showman can make a pretty productive pair. *Vive la différence!*

upehor leisurely ... considered modest

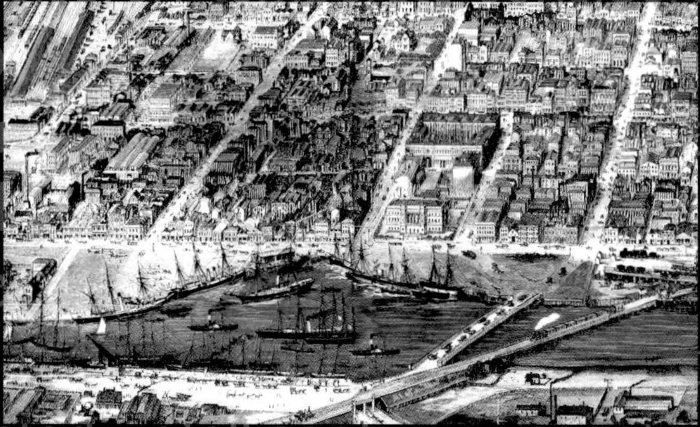

rivate so ... iet dowdy

houghtfu ... e educated

wowseris ... regal slow

uality te ... scholarly

eserved ... ull bolshy

ophisticated intelligent wowserish moderate

ubdued quiet classy stylish elitist cosmopolitan

sydney vs melbourne

avish exuberant fast brawny sharp convict

ublic new money gaudy loud immediate

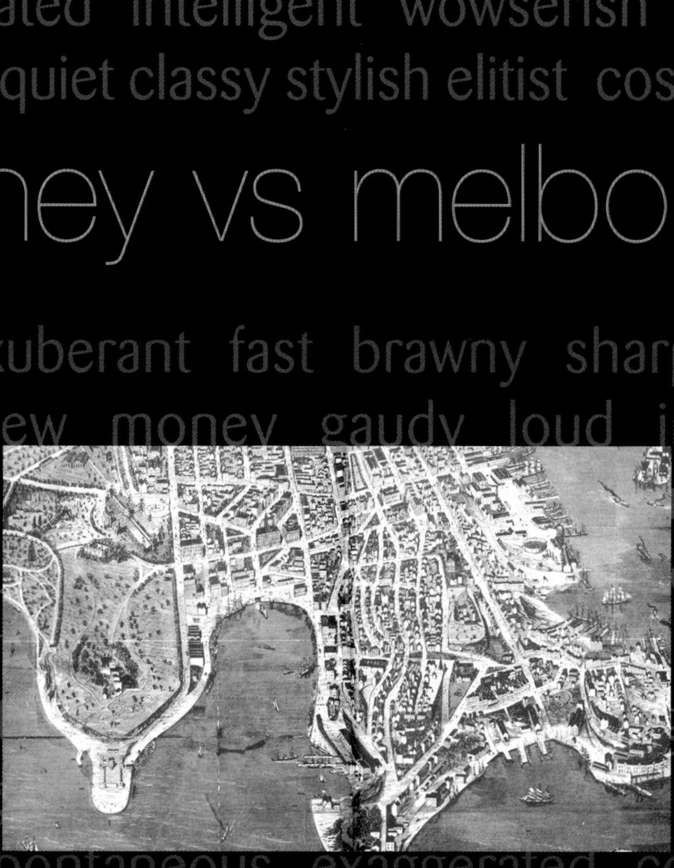

xtrovert ... ick pushy

noney hu ... er shallow

onvict s ... confident

asy hust ... ger money

hallow g ... gung-ho

rassy spontaneous exaggerated commercial

kerry

armstrong

"Melbourne seems to thrive on a deep-seated modesty, while Sydney seems to thrive on exactly the opposite."

1934

heide

THE FIRST
MUSEUM OF MODERN ART
IN AUSTRALIA

Centre & Right: Copyright Estate of Albert Tucker Courtesy Lauraine Diggins Fine Art & Heide Museum of Mode

Truncated in perfect Aussie slang from Heidelberg to 'Heide', this was the country homestead of wealthy Melbourne socialite Sunday Baillieu and her equally wealthy lawyer husband John Reed. In the sparsely populated Melbourne of the 1930s, Heidelberg was still a rural idyll. Set in rolling green dairy pasture by the banks of the meandering upper Yarra, Heide offered ideal sanctuary for reflection, creation and inspiration. Here the Reeds built a home and indulged their passion for art and life. They invited artists, musicians and writers to share their home, their wealth and their possessions. They talked ideas, politics, art and music and explored life's gristly themes. In their profound generosity, the Reeds nurtured and sustained creative minds and bodies alike. They created a space, both physical and intellectual, in which artists could create. To some, like John Perceval, Joy Hester and Albert Tucker, they also paid a stipend in exchange for their paintings. This rich cooperation made Heide the home of modern art in Australia in the 1930s and 40s, with many of the significant works of Australia's modern art created here.

The close proximity of their intermingled lives as well as the seclusion of Heide and the heightened passions and politics of the times all combined to fuel a unique creativity of expression. Sadly it also bore some unplanned and tragic consequences. Along with the art came explosive relationships, love triangles, infidelity and abandonment, in a set of relationships as intense and complex as the paintings themselves.

Max Harris
1921–

Writer and Poet. From 1940 was publisher of the *Angry Penguins* magazine from which the group takes its name.

Sidney Nolan
1917–1992

Son of a Melbourne tram driver, Nolan spent nine years at Heide, where he painted all but one of his Ned Kelly series. Nolan hid out at Heide at times after he deserted from the army. Had famous affair with Sunday while living with the Reeds. Became the favourite protégé of the Reeds. Left Heide and soon married John Reed's sister Cynthia Reed which shattered Sunday. As Nolan's success increased, he tried to dissociate himself from the Reeds. A year after Cynthia's death, Nolan married Mary Boyd, John Perceval's ex-wife. This sparked the fury of Patrick White – a great friend of Cynthia Reed – and began a long feud between White and Nolan.

Sunday Reed
1905–1980

Born a Baillieu, Sunday Reed was first cousin of Dame Merlyn (Baillieu) Myer, wife of Sidney Myer. Sunday married John Reed and settled at Heide. Patron of the arts and generous hostess, she was the driving creative spirit at Heide. She was notable, too, for her affairs. She had a relationship with Sam Atyeo, as did her sister-in-law Cynthia, and one with Sidney Nolan, who later became Cynthia's husband. Sunday's first marriage had left her infertile through infection, although she later adopted Joy Hester's son Sweeney in 1949 after Hester abandoned her marriage to Tucker. Sunday died at Heide, just 10 days after John's death.

John Reed
1901–1980

Cambridge-educated Tasmanian grazier's son. Lawyer and patron of the arts, he lobbied generously on behalf of his artists, tirelessly promoting them to newspapers, galleries and likely patrons. He saw himself as the catalyst between the artist and their audience. Reed favoured Sidney Nolan and his work, and it was said that he wanted Nolan's mind as much as Sunday wanted his love. In 1980, the Reeds sold their homestead and part of their art collection to the Victorian government, and donated a generous endowment for the museum. It is John Reed's spidery script of the museum's name that is used as a logo today.

Joy Hester
1920–60

'Soulsister' of Sunday Reed. Joy Hester was an accomplished artist, the only female in the Angry Penguins. She married Albert Tucker, although renowned for her many affairs. She exhibited widely from the first Contemporary Art Show of 1939, including three solo exhibitions in the 1950s. When she left Tucker for her lover (artist Gray Smith) in 1947 Hester 'gave' her two-year-old son Sweeney to the childless Sunday Reed. Hester and Smith had a son, Peregrine, and a daughter, Fern. Diagnosed with Hodgkin's disease, Hester died at just 40 years old.

Sweeney Reed
1945–1979

Son of Joy Hester and Albert Tucker, (although his father was later reported to be a famous Melbourne jazz drummer). Sweeney was an unwanted child who was eventually 'given' to the childless and wealthy Reeds to raise as their own son at Heide. He lived the unpredictable life of a child surrounded by adults who could not find a place for him in their complex lives. As a young man, Sweeney worked as a gallery director, and was once described as 'the Andy Warhol of Melbourne'. He had two children with his second wife, Pamela Westh. Sweeney committed suicide by drug overdose at the age of 34 in 1979.

Albert Tucker
1914–1999

Successful modernist expressionist painter. Explored the trauma and dark themes of the Depression and of war in his work. Self taught, he was the first to make his work pay in Australia while others needed to trek to London to find success.

Danila Vassilieff
1897–1958

Described as the 'dashing cossack', this Russian refugee artist settled in Melbourne in 1935. The Reeds enjoyed the energy and passion in both the man and his expressionist paintings.

Cynthia Reed
1908–1976

John Reed's sister, Cynthia, was a close friend of Sydney writer Patrick White. She had an affair with Sam Atyeo, and later married Sidney Nolan, the former lover of her sister-in-law, Sunday Reed. Their marriage ended any happy contact between Nolan and the Reeds at Heide. She had a daughter Jinx, who was adopted by Nolan after his marriage to Cynthia. Cynthia suicided in 1976.

Arthur Boyd
1920–1999

Expressionist painter. Parents and grandparents were artists. Was conscripted into the army in 1941 where he met Perceval, Nolan and Tucker.

Mary Boyd
1926–

Artist. Married John Perceval. Member of influential bohemian family of artists, the Boyds of Murrumbeena, including Guy, Arthur, Mary and Lucy, children of potter and sculptor Merric Boyd, and painter Emma. Mary Boyd married Sidney Nolan after Cynthia Reed's death.

John Perceval
1923–2000

Artist, ceramicist, sculptor. The longest-lived of the Angry Penguins, his real name was Linwood South. Born in W.A., he changed his name when he moved to Melbourne in 1934.

Mirka Mora
1928–

Artist Mora and her art dealer husband Georges were regular visitors to Heide. Owners of Cafe Mirka, Cafe Balzac, Tolarno restaurant and Tolarno Gallery. Mora has sons Philippe, William, Tyriel - all of whom played as children with a young Sweeney Reed amidst the complexities of creative parents, parties and painting at Heide. Philippe is director of the story of Heide *When we were Modern*.

Sam Atyeo
1910–1990

Artist and furniture designer. Had affair with Cynthia Reed. Friend and eventually personal assistant to Herbert 'Doc' Evatt, high profile lawyer, leader of the ALP and president of the first UN General Assembly. Atyeo was known as Evatt's trusted confidante.

Barrett Reid
1926–1995

Modern art critic, writer, poet. Was granted lifetime tenure in 1981 at the original Heide homestead after the Reeds' deaths.

Charles Blackman
1928–

Renowned artist, Blackman frequently visited Heide with his wife Barbara.

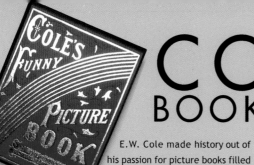

COLE'S
BOOK ARCADE

E.W. Cole made history out of his passion for picture books filled with fun and playful nonsense. Devoted to the task, he rarely played or read with his own children or grandchildren, who remember him as a kindly, mild-mannered but rather self-sufficient man. Yet he created a lifetime of children's entertainment that has lasted over 130 years.

Lured from England by the goldfields, he soon turned instead to selling lemonade, then pies, then second-hand books. Cole was transfixed by life's big questions. Drawing on his wide readings of everything from the Bible to Charles Darwin he designed his own philosophy and eventually resolved to publish his own books. Buying and selling books to pay his way, he created the most famous Melbourne landmark of his time.

Cole's Book Arcade of Bourke Street in 1874 was indeed the 'Grandest Bookshop in the World'. Designed as a long, narrow arcade, it was littered with amusing signs and posters encouraging people to read for hours among the stacks of books and the eccentric collection of curios and bric-a-brac. Gaslights blazed among the potted palms and wicker chairs, and the heart of Bourke Street sparkled invitingly.

The first *Funny Picture Book* edition of 1879 is still in print today. Cole packaged up his home-grown wisdom into these volumes that he subtitled 'Family Amuser or Instructor', and 'Intellect Sharpener'. He lightened their presentation with picture puzzles, riddles and nonsense poems. He added historic prose, classical references, travelogues of exotic lands and peoples and tall-tales-and-true. Into this mix he placed sentimental odes to the sanctity and beauty of women, children and family. He offered morality lessons on the brotherhood of man and the ignorance of racism, the perils of loose living and the magnificence of common sense.

He also designed his own style of advertising, creating hoax news stories that Melburnians loved to read, and causing *Melbourne Herald* sales to soar as never before. He invited, incited, and dared people to read. He seduced them into reading through his clever advertising campaigns. He tricked them into deeper thinking through the harmless lure of comics. He dropped promotional 'coins' all over Melbourne streets which could be redeemed for gifts at his store. He designed a rainbow logo to signify all races coming together as one under the banner of knowledge. The mega book-stores of today would not come close to the tactics of this, the original 'concept bookstore'.

Cole advertised for a wife in an open letter in the *Melbourne Herald*. What's more, he found her, they married and lived happily together. He swapped seedpods with the first director of the Botanic Gardens, Baron Ferdinand von Mueller. His antics were the talk of Melbourne. Like many of his peers he was an inspirational combination of entrepreneur and socialist, who did big business with a big heart.

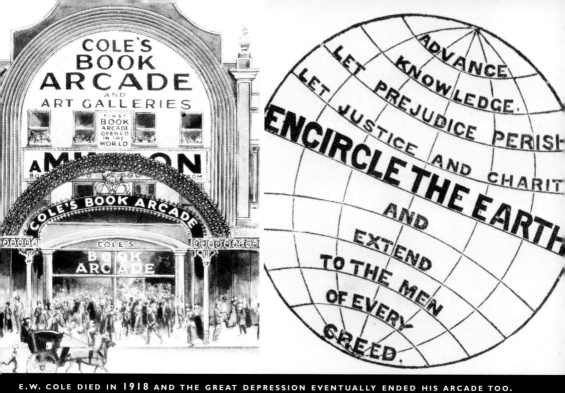

COLE'S BOOK ARCADE AND ART GALLERIES

FIRST BOOK ARCADE OPENED IN THE WORLD

ADVANCE KNOWLEDGE. LET PREJUDICE PERISH. LET JUSTICE AND CHARITY ENCIRCLE THE EARTH AND EXTEND TO THE MEN OF EVERY CREED.

E.W. COLE DIED IN 1918 AND THE GREAT DEPRESSION EVENTUALLY ENDED HIS ARCADE TOO. HIS DAUGHTER LINDA, GRANDSON COLE TURNLEY AND GREAT-GRANDDAUGHTER MERRON KEPT THE FUNNY PICTURE BOOKS ALIVE AND IN PRINT FOR OVER 130 YEARS.

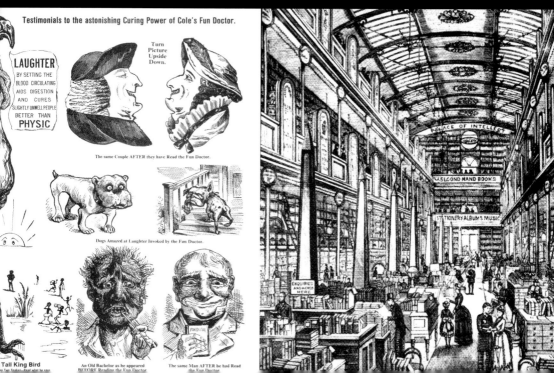

Testimonials to the astonishing Curing Power of Cole's Fun Doctor.

LAUGHTER BY SETTING THE BLOOD CIRCULATING AIDS DIGESTION AND CURES SLIGHTLY UNWELL PEOPLE BETTER THAN **PHYSIC**

Turn Picture Upside Down.

The same Couple AFTER they have Read the Fun Doctor.

Dogs Amazed at Laughter Invoked by the Fun Doctor.

Tall King Bird

An Old Bachelor as he appeared BEFORE Reading the Fun Doctor

The same Man AFTER he had Read the Fun Doctor

"BOOKS ARE EMBLEMS OF PEACE ON EARTH."

E.W. COLE

MELBOURNE'S GAMES

footy

Australian Rules Football is the game of the people. Born right here, it is Melbourne's own.

A 'real man's' game, it is full of strategy, muscle and guts. It's earthy, macho and bloody-nosed.

That's probably why it's not commonly known that the inventor of the game was the wealthy, cricket-loving son of a Queensland squatter, whose tragic life ended in suicide.

The Father of Aussie Rules, Thomas Wills enjoyed a privileged childhood, and was reportedly greatly embarrassed by his grandfather's former convict status. As the son of a colonial pastoralist, he was sent to England for his education, at Rugby College. And like most young men of his class and time, cricket was his first sporting love.

In 1856 when Wills returned to his home in Melbourne, he was concerned about Melbourne's cricketers becoming flabby in the winter months between cricket seasons. It was Wills' idea to play some kind of football in the intervening months, and he and his cousin Harrison designed a unique combination of Gaelic football and rugby that produced a more skillful football style that was not quite as rough and damaging as rugby.

Football gained in popularity in Melbourne. Some say locals already played a game much like today's, some say it even has indigenous origins. A match between St Kilda Grammar and Melbourne Grammar held on the St Kilda foreshore in June 1858 is the first on any school records, with St Kilda winning the match. In July the same year, Tom Wills umpired a match between rival schools Scotch College and Melbourne Grammar.

With 40 players a side, a huge round ball, and goal posts 1.6 km apart, it was held in a Richmond paddock, now the site of the carpark at the hallowed Melbourne Cricket Ground. Play lasted from noon until dark, with one goal to Scotch, and was continued a fortnight later when Melbourne Grammar scored a goal. The following week the tie-breaker was played, but with no further advancement in the score, it was declared a draw. Rules were subsequently drawn up in 1859 for the Australian Rules code by cricketers Wills, Hammersley, Bruce, Smith, Butterworth and Sewell. Melbourne has been home to Aussie Rules football ever since, now fitting cricket in between the footy seasons.

Wills was the driving force in the invention of this unique code, in the establishment of regular games, and in the organisation and administration of early club affairs. But just three years after his famous first game was played, his life took a tragic turn.

In 1861 his father and three brothers were killed by Aborigines in a brutal massacre on his father's station in remote outback Queensland. Wills was delayed by wagon breakdown on his return to the property, and so escaped the attack, which was soon avenged when police killed approximately 60 Aborigines in a frenzied retaliation.

Wills returned to Victoria and, remarkably, began an association with Aboriginal cricketers. He went on to compose an all-Aboriginal cricket side which was in fact the very first Australian cricket team. Wills toured the team through England in 1868.

Wills was deeply traumatised by the death of his father, and in his later years battled against depression and alcoholism. He was eventually treated at Kew Asylum, and later stabbed himself to death with scissors at his Heidelberg home in 1880.

Back Row: TARPOT.   T.W. WILLS (Capt.).   MULLAGH.
Row: KING COLE(Standing). JELLICOE. PETER. RED CAP. HARRY ROSE. BULLOCKY. CUZENS. DICK A DICK(Standing).

...ter sculptor Louis Laumen eloquently gives us
...gift of our own game in the form of a frozen
...nent, 150 years old. Tom Wills appears as
...ire behind two of Melbourne's earliest players.
... sculpture was commissioned in 2001 by ancient
...ls Scotch college and Melbourne Grammar to
...memorate the 150th anniversary of their first
...e together in 1858. The final bronze now
...nds at the MCG.

183

cricket & footy

In Melbourne, football is inevitable. Melbourne is football-mad. As long as the blood of human multitudes is gushing through the turnstiles of Melbourne's central sporting organ, the MCG, all's well with the world.

Polls vary, tastes change, and new populations constantly alter the weight of public support and preference for other codes, but Australian Rules footy reigns supreme. In Melbourne, football and cricket have been joined since birth by their shared home — the Melbourne Cricket Ground. This one place is both the sacred site of football in winter and a magnet to cricket addicts in summer. Footy began as the seasonal flip side to cricket, and they are inseparable on the city's calendar; the yin and yang of Melbourne's sporting philosophy. But Australian Rules rules Melbourne. It rules the air space, the virtual space, and it also rules the actual space. Melbourne boasts no less than 101 football ovals and cricket pitches in inner Melbourne alone. And in greater Melbourne there are more footy ovals and cricket pitches (over 2150) than there are churches or schools. Which is not ideal, but in Melbourne sport is certainly a religion, and always an education.

Although begun by Melbourne's aristocracy, football has always been tagged the people's game. But any illusion that the people ever owned the game has been shortlived. Sport in general and football in particular are today more than ever the province of corporate giants, and the stakes are the billions involved in sponsorship, marketing and promotion. Sophisticated, manicured, and manipulated by big media

business, the game has certainly changed since 1858.

In the beginning, footy's original teams were Melbourne, formed in 1858 (and still going as the AFL's oldest club), Geelong in 1859, South Yarra in 1860, Carlton, Royal Park and Albert Park (later South Melbourne) all in 1864, Brunswick in 1865, and Hotham (later North Melbourne) in 1869. Still other clubs had names now long forgotten, like University, Warehouseman's, Southern Imperial Melbourne, Young Victorians, and Rising Sun.

The Victorian Football Association (VFA) was formed in 1877, and things took their first turn towards the mercenary in 1896, when the eight most popular clubs split off in a push to cut out weaker clubs and thereby increase their share of the gate's takings. They set up the Victorian Football League (VFL), which reigned until 1990. They were Carlton, Collingwood, Essendon, St Kilda, South Melbourne, Fitzroy, Geelong and Melbourne. Richmond and University joined in 1908, with University winding up in 1914. In 1924, Hawthorn, Footscray and North Melbourne were also admitted to the VFL.

The nationalisation of the game from VFL to Australian Football League (AFL) in 1990 has led to Melbourne's game becoming national property. Teams were signed, sold and sent to far flung states as the AFL took the game away from home for the first time. South Melbourne's Swans became Sydney's Swans, Brisbane formed the Bears (later mutating into the Brisbane Lions after the injection of Melbourne's Fitzroy team), and Perth produced the Westcoast Eagles and the

IN MELBOURNE THERE ARE MORE FOOTY OVALS AND CRICKET PITCHES THAN CHURCHES OR SCHOOLS. BUT THEN FOOTY'S CERTAINLY A RELIGION, AND ALWAYS AN EDUCATION.

Fremantle Dockers. In 1991 Adelaide's Crows landed. Fitzroy moved north to join Brisbane in 1996, and Port Adelaide entered the AFL in 1997. All of which brought the unthinkable to pass — preliminary final games played by non-Melbourne teams held outside Victoria, at an arena other than the MCG. The MCG is contracted to hold all grand finals for the next 40 years, but the politics of where grand finals are played may well provide much debate in years to come should non-Melbourne teams prove to be regular winners.

Back in the 1950s and 60s, Melburnians really were all footy warriors; when Dad's team was your team, and local clubs truly coloured their neighbourhoods. Today, it's far less tribal, and harder to be loyal. Teams are merged or dissolved, and fans are not considered in decisions to close clubs and trade players. Local grounds are destined to disappear, as one by one, home parks are sold up to real estate developers.

New mega-arenas now threaten the domination of Melbourne's sporting cathedral, the Melbourne Cricket Ground. From 1961 to 1995, the MCG held the world record for the largest crowd at a cricket match — 90,800, topping that with football grand final crowds of 100,000. But in August 2000 for the first time ever, a Melbourne international one-day cricket match was played, not at the MCG, but at the more recent rival stadium at Docklands.

Today there are around 77,000 members of the Melbourne Cricket Club and another 166,000 on the waiting list. And the MCG, Melbourne's greatest sporting icon, is built almost entirely from membership funds. Apart from a £100,000 contribution from the

government towards an Olympic improvement in 1956, and the imminent 2006 Commonwealth Games upgrade, all funds to build and maintain the MCG have come from the members themselves. And yet they do not own the MCG, and the Melbourne Cricket Club has no guaranteed tenure at the ground.

Apart from club rooms and team training areas, the MCG currently houses dining halls, function rooms, an Olympic museum, a library, and a cricket museum. The museum boasts one of the finest collections of sporting memorabilia in the country, and the library houses an extensive collection and vast sporting archive. Chosen as the athletics track and venue for opening and closing ceremonies for the Melbourne Commonwealth Games of 2006, the MCG is set to undergo a $500 million upgrade including the demolition of the historic Members' Pavilion, the Library and legendary Long Room.

Melburnians talk footy politics with the same passion that they talk football play. Love it or hate it, it's inescapable. But as it is increasingly removed from its grass roots, Australian Rules footy is under threat. Soccer, popular with Australia's Asian and European migrants, is increasing its audience, while simultaneously being wooed by local politicians eager to stage a lucrative World Cup.

Like Vegemite, Australian Rules Football has been cherished in isolation by its devoted fans. It has enjoyed pride of place for 150 years. Having traded in 100 per cent loyalty in Victoria to take its chances against national and international codes, the new game for Australian Rules will be to find its place in a very big pond.

LEST WE FORGET
1914 · 18
M.C.C. MEMBERS WHO MADE THE SUPR

1907
T WARNE
P McALISTER (CAPT)
C McKENZIE
F TARRANT
V S RANSFORD
J HORAN
C R HAZLITT
A V CARROLL
W CARKEEK
F COLLINS
J V SAUNDERS

187

The labels on the diagram read:

Northern Stand 2002-2006
Members' Pavilion 1928
1881
1854
Olympic Stand 1956
1884
1877
Grey Smith 1906
Western Ponsford Stand 1967
Concrete Stand 1926
Mellowrne Cricket Ground
Harrison 1908
Great Southern Stand 1991
Open Wooden 1900
Southern Stand 1936
Wardill Stand 1912

GRANDSTANDS AT THE MCG

Members' Stand #1 1854, removed and sold to the Richmond Cricket Club for £55 in 1881, replaced by:

Members' Stand #2 1881, demolished 1927 and replaced by:

Members' Stand #3 1928–2006

Northern Stand #1 1877, destroyed by fire 1884, replaced by:

Northern Stand #2 1884, demolished and replaced by:

Olympic Stand 1956–2006

Grey Smith Stand 1906, demolished in 1966 to make way for new Western/ Ponsford Stand

Concrete Stand 1926, also demolished in 1966 and replaced by:

Western/Ponsford Stand 1967–2006

Olympic Stand, Members' Pavilion, and Western/Ponsford Stand, to be replaced by new Northern Stand for the 2006 Commonwealth Games.

Harrison Stand 1908, demolished 1936 for the building of the Southern Stand

Wardill Stand 1912, also demolished in 1936 for Southern Stand

Open Wooden Stand 1900, demolished in 1936 for Southern Stand

Southern Stand 1936–37 demolished 1990 to make way for Great Southern Stand

Great Southern Stand 1991–curr

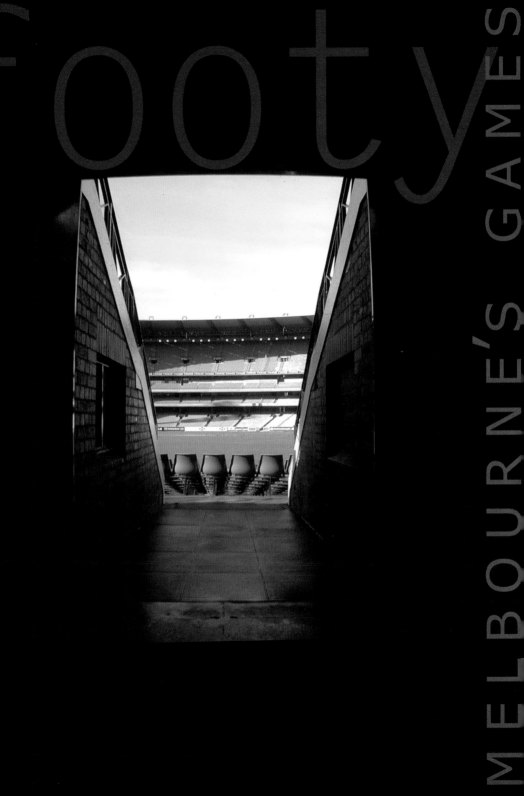

footy

MELBOURNE'S GAMES

vince colos

actor

> **"** Melbourne in a word? Passionate.
> There's an undercurrent always there,
> whether it's footy or art or politics...
> even eating. The value is under the
> surface here. It's deep. Very deep. **"**

imo

such is life, I shall see you where'd go, su su she see you where'd go, su shall see you where'd go su an is life go i sha ra see you whe life go, such is life

NED KELLY

Why do we revere a bandit and a murderer? Why does Ned Kelly retain such hero status? Victoria's 1800s were beset by more than one bushranger, preying on gentler folk by petty thieving and not-so-petty assault and robbery. It was not an honourable day's work. It was often the resort of cowards and villains. So why celebrate Ned? Circumstances can excuse many a rogue, and he was certainly born to a time that presented cowards and villains in police uniforms as well as bushranger's gear. He was also born to a proud family that taught him not to kowtow to jumped-up authority, and there was plenty of that. But there is a difference to Ned's career. He earned a mythical status for earthly reasons. Ned Kelly robbed banks and not other settlers' homesteads, shops or wagons. And further, while inside one of these banks with the safe door open, he seized the moment and burned the mortgage deeds to small settlements in the area, freeing struggling families from debt. That's bound to win you friends. And there's more...His youth and innocence at the beginning and his death at just 25 years of age, his fierce loyalty, his defiance in court, his stoic conviction that he did no wrong, his theatrical performance at his last stand, his innate understanding of the power of public performance, his colourful Irish turn of phrase, his creativity, wit and keen intelligence, his marvellous 'Jerilderie' letter to the press and of course — his inventive armour. Through this 'superhero's' suit he turned the most masterly public relations manouevre of our history, creating a powerful visual symbol that melds all these attributes into one. For Australians, this powerful graphic icon is right up there with those of Che Guevara and even Jesus, and it is no accident his mighty persona overshadows any Batman or Burke, or even Buckley. The image of his armour, especially as stylised by Sidney Nolan, connects us in an instant with the idea of courage and cause, and his 'battler' status still resonates loud and clear with each repetition of this symbol. As piece after piece of his armour is recovered — even into the 21st century — it distills Ned the man into an idea that, as it gets simpler, seems to speak louder, become more robust, and inspire generation after generation.

Subject of the world's first full-length feature film, *The Story of the Kelly Gang*, made in Melbourne in 1906

THE SENTENCING OF NED KELLY

The jury then retired, and after deliberating about half-an-hour returned into Court with a verdict of guilty.

The prisoner, [**NED KELLY**]*, having been asked in the usual way if he had any statement to make, said:–* Well, it is rather too late for me to speak now. I thought of speaking this morning and all day, but there was little use, and there is little use blaming anyone now. Nobody knew about my case except myself, and I wish I had insisted on being allowed to examine the witnesses myself. If I had examined them, I am confident I would have thrown a different light on the case. It is not that I fear death; I fear it as little as to drink a cup of tea. On the evidence that has been given, no juryman could have given any other verdict. That is my opinion. But as I say, if I had examined the witnesses I would have shown matters in a different light, because no man understands the case as I do myself. I do not blame anybody — neither Mr Bindon nor Mr Gaunson; but Mr Bindon knew nothing about my case. I lay blame on myself that I did not get up yesterday and examine the witnesses, but I thought that if I did so it would look like bravado and flashness.

The court crier having called upon all to observe a strict silence whilst the judge pronounced the awful sentence of death,

HIS HONOUR [JUDGE SIR REDMOND BARRY] said:– Edward Kelly, the verdict pronounced by the jury is one which you must have fully expected.

THE PRISONER: Yes, under the circumstances.

HIS HONOUR: No circumstances that I can conceive could have altered the result of your trial.

THE PRISONER: Perhaps not from what you can now conceive, but if you had heard me examine the witnesses it would have been different.

HIS HONOUR: I will give you full credit for all the skill you appear to desire to assume.

THE PRISONER: No, I don't wish to assume anything. There is no flashness or bravado about me. It is not that I want to save my life, because I know I would have been capable of clearing myself of the charge, and I could have saved my life in spite of all against me.

HIS HONOUR: The facts are so numerous, and so convincing, not only as regards the original offence with which you are charged, but with respect to a long series of transactions covering a period of 18 months, that no rational person would

BIG NED
AT GLENROWAN'S
POST OFFICE

hesitate to arrive at any other conclusion but that the verdict of the jury is irresistible, and that it is right. I have no desire whatever to inflict upon you any personal remarks. It is not becoming that I should endeavour to aggravate the sufferings with which your mind must be sincerely agitated.

THE PRISONER: No, I don't think that. My mind is as easy as the mind of any man in this world as I am prepared to show before God and man.

HIS HONOUR: It is blasphemous for you to say that. You appear to revel in the idea of having put men to death.

THE PRISONER: More men than me have put men to death, but I am the last man in the world that would take a man's life. Two years ago, even if my own life was at stake, and I am confident if I thought a man would shoot me, I would give him a chance of keeping his life, and would part rather with my own. But if I knew that through him innocent persons' lives were at stake I certainly would have to shoot him if he forced me to do so, but I would want to know that he was really going to take innocent life.

HIS HONOUR: Your statement involves a cruelly wicked charge of perjury against a phalanx of witnesses.

THE PRISONER: I daresay, but a day will come at a bigger court than this when we shall see which is right and which is wrong. No matter how long a man lives, he is bound to come to judgment somewhere, and as well here as anywhere. It will be different the next time they have a Kelly trial, for they are not all killed. It would have been for the good of the Crown had I examined the witnesses; and I would have stopped a lot of the reward, I can assure you; and I do not know but I will do it yet, if allowed.

HIS HONOUR: An offence of this kind is of no ordinary character. Murders had been discovered which had been committed under circumstances of great atrocity. They proceeded from motives other than that which actuated you. They have had their origin in many sources. Some have been committed from a sordid desire to take from others the property they had aquired, some from jealousy, some from a desire for revenge, but yours is a more aggravated crime, and one of larger proportions, for with a party of men you took up arms against society, organised as it is for mutual protection, and for respect of law.

"IT IS NOT THAT I FEAR DEATH; I FEAR

Argus.

OCTOBER 30, 1880.

REPORTED IN THE ARGUS NEWSPAPER

THE PRISONER: That is the way the evidence came out here. It appeared that I deliberately took up arms of my own accord, and induced the other three men to join me for the purpose of doing nothing but shooting down the police.

HIS HONOUR: In new communities, where the bonds of society are not so well linked together as in older countries, there is unfortunately a class which disregards the evil consequences of crime. Foolish, inconsiderate, ill-conducted, unprincipled youths unfortunately abound, and unless they are made to consider the consequences of crime they are led to imitate notorious felons, whom they regard as self-made heroes. It is right therefore that they should be asked to consider and reflect upon what the life of a felon is. A felon who has cut himself off from all decencies, all the affections, charities, and all the obligations of society is as helpless and degraded as a wild beast of the field. He has nowhere to lay his head, he has no one to prepare for him the comforts of life, he suspects his friends, he dreads his enemies, he is in constant alarm lest his pursuers should reach him, and his only hope is that he might use his life in what he considers a glorious struggle for existence. That is the life of the outlaw or felon, and it would be well for those young men who are so foolish as to consider that it is brave of a man to sacrifice the lives of his fellow-creatures in carrying out his own wild ideas, to see that it is a life to be avoided by every possible means, and to reflect that the unfortunate termination of your life is a miserable death. New South Wales joined with Victoria in providing ample inducement to persons to assist in having you and your companions apprehended, but by some spell which I cannot understand – a spell which exists in all lawless communities more or less – which may be attributed either to a sympathy for outlaws, or a dread of the consequences which would result from the performance of their duty – no persons were found who would be tempted by the reward. The love of country, the love of order, the love of obedience to law, have been set aside for reasons difficult to explain, and there is something extremely wrong in a country where a lawless band of men are able to live for 18 months disturbing society. During your short life you have stolen, according to your own statements, over 200 horses.

THE PRISONER: Who proves that?

HIS HONOUR: More than one witness has testified that you made the statement on several occasions.

THE PRISONER: That charge has never been proved against me, and it is held in English law that a man is innocent until he is found guilty.

HIS HONOUR: You are self-accused. The statement was made voluntarily by yourself. Then you and your companions committed attacks on two banks, and appropriated therefrom large sums of money, amounting to several thousands of pounds. Further, I cannot conceal from myself the fact that an expenditure of £50,000 has been necessary in consequence of the acts with which you and your party have been connected. We have had samples of felons and their [c]areers, such as those of Bradl[e]y and O'Connor, Clark, Gardiner, Melville, Morgan, Scott, and Smith, all of whom have come to ignominious deaths; still the effect expected from their punishment has not been produced. This is much to be deplored. When such examples as these are so often repeated society must be reorganised, or it must soon be seriously affected. Your unfortunate and miserable companions have died a death which probably you might rather envy, but you are not afforded the opportunity—

THE PRISONER: I don't think there is much proof that they did die that death.

HIS HONOUR: In your case the law will be carried out by its offices. The gentlemen of the jury have done their duty. My duty will be to forward to the proper quarter the notes of your trial and to lay, as I am required to do, before the Executive any circumstances connected with your trial that may be required. I can hold out to you no hope. I do not see that I can entertain the slightest reason for saying you can expect anything. I desire to spare you any more pain, and I absolve myself from any of my utterances that may have unnecessarily increased the agitation of your mind. I have now to pronounce your sentence.

HIS HONOUR then sentenced the prisoner to death in the usual form, ending with the usual words, 'May the Lord have mercy on your soul.'

THE PRISONER: I will go a little further than that, and say I will see you there where I go.

The court was cleared, and the prisoner was removed to the Melbourne gaol.

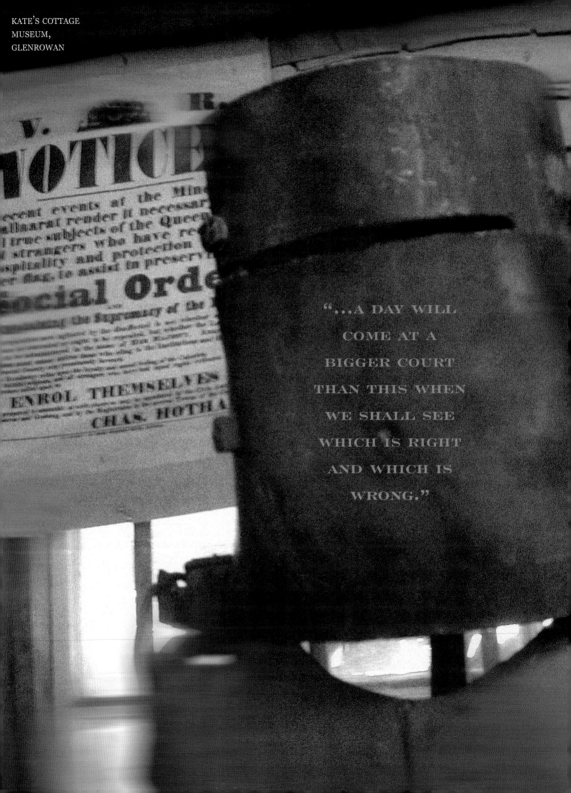

"...A DAY WILL COME AT A BIGGER COURT THAN THIS WHEN WE SHALL SEE WHICH IS RIGHT AND WHICH IS WRONG."

The Queen must surely be proud of such heroic men as the Police and Irish soldiers as it takes eight or eleven of the biggest mud-crushers in Melbourne to take one poor little half starved larrikin to a watchhouse. I have seen as many as eleven big and ugly enough to lift Mount Macedon out of a crab hole – more like the species of a baboon or gorilla than a man – actually come into a court house and swear they could not arrest one eight stone larrikin (and them armed with batons and neddies) without some civilian assistance and some of them going to the hospital from the effects of hits from the fists of the larrikin and the magistrate would send the poor little larrikin into a dungeon for being a better man than such a parcel of armed curs.

'But they must remember those men came into the bush with the intention of scattering pieces of me and my brother all over the bush and yet they know and acknowledge I have been wronged and my mother and four or five men lagged innocent.

'And is my mother and brothers and sisters not to be pitied also who has no alternative but to put up with the brutal and cowardly conduct of a parcel of big ugly fat-necked wombat-headed big-bellied magpie-legged narrow-hipped splaw-footed sons of Irish bailiffs or English landlords which is better known as Officers of Justice or the Victorian Police?

'It will pay Government to give those people who are suffering Innocence Justice and Liberty. If not I will be compelled to show some colonial stratagem which will open the eyes of not only the Victoria Police force and inhabitants but also the whole British army and no doubt they will acknowledge their hounds were barking at the wrong stump.

"

Edward 'Ned' Kelly
'Jerilderie Letter'

The eight-hour day was invented in Melbourne.

8 hours rest ⏰ 8 hours labour ⏰ 8 hours recreation

It has an almost Biblical rhythm to it; a natural logic. Fought for and won by the stonemasons of Melbourne in 1856, it was the foundation of the union movement's aim to secure a 40-hour working week (or 44 with Saturday mornings) and its protection has been a constant theme of labour battles ever since. ⏰ The union claimed there was more to life than toiling for a day's pay. They argued that time should be set aside to enjoy the good things in life like family, fun, friends. Time for the improvement of one's own mind and body was argued to be worthy of official protection. It's a wonderful notion that seems to have been lost over the decades. ⏰ Today, all that remains is a faint memory of a more generous, family-friendly rhythm, and a tired, over-worked feeling. And near Trades Hall, this cryptic monument to the three great privileges of life: work, rest and play.

ELBOURNE HAS BEEN HOME TO LABOUR MOVEMENTS AND WORKERS' STRUGGLES FROM S VERY EARLIEST. TWO YEARS BEFORE THE EIGHT-HOUR MOVEMENT, THE REBELLION AT HE EUREKA STOCKADE WAS FOUGHT ON THE GOLDFIELDS IN 1854. THIS UPRISING EFLECTED THE IMPORTED POLITICS OF IRISH AND EUROPEAN WORKERS WHO WERE ETERMINED TO GET A FAIR GO OUT OF THIS NEW FRONTIER AND WHO CHALLENGED THE D ORDER TO THE DEATH TO DO SO. THE AUSTRALIAN TASTE FOR DEMOCRATIC RIGHTS AS NURTURED — SOME SAY BORN — AT EUREKA, AND BROUGHT BACK TO MELBOURNE IN HE BREASTS OF IMMIGRANT MINERS WHO STAYED ON AND MADE MELBOURNE THEIR HOME.

The ute

'The ute is more than just a car. The ute is a thing of beauty. The ute is part of our national identity. The ute is an expression of one's lifestyle. The ute makes boys into men.'

Sam Ritchie, Ute Appreciation Society of Australia

As all Ute lovers know, the Ute is a way of life. Born near Melbourne in Geelong, it was designed for a demanding bush lifestyle, but was embraced by city dwellers and lives on today delivering lifestyle solutions to thousands of city and rural devotees. According to the Ute Appreciation Society, utes fall into four categories. The City Ute is a showcar, used to work and to 'pull chicks' and is always maintained in immaculate condition. The Work Ute, however, must be parked badly and treated with casual contempt. It should be devoid of any comfort options, these being replaced by rubbish, rust and tools. The Country Ute is a combination 'chick-magnet and mobile home', making it the centre of its owner's rural universe, while the Feral Ute is a clapped-out shooter's ute with no matching panels, no muffler, and definitely no registration.

This world of flexibility is the result of a Gippsland farmer's wife who wrote to the Ford Motor Company in 1932 and asked for a car that could haul pigs throughout the week, and take her family to church on Sundays. Not a truck, not a car, but a combination of both. To avoid the weakness of a centre-joined chassis, 22-year-old Lew Bandt at Ford Geelong designed an entirely new rear section that was integrated with the roof and sides of the car. He created the world's first ever sedan-based utility, on the road by 1934, and made the drive from the bush to the big smoke of Melbourne a thrill. He went on to design a station wagon, ambulances, and the first Falcon ute. Back in the USA, a delighted Henry Ford dubbed the Ute a 'kangaroo chaser'. But as we now know, it's so much more than that. From a 'tidy XF' popular among probationary drivers out to impress, to an XY GT replica, 'lowered and worked', the Ute offers endless possibilities. The all new XL is a machine no woman could resist, its sleek new lines demanding hours of buffing, polishing and love, until eventually, another boy becomes a man.

A TRIBUTE

INVENTOR OF THE UTE, LEW BANDT, DIED NOT ONLY
IN A UTE, BUT IN *THE* UTE — A REPLICA OF HIS
1934 ORIGINAL. HE CRASHED IT IN 1987 WHILE
DRIVING TO A DOCUMENTARY SHOOT LOCATION TO
MAKE A FILM ABOUT...THE BIRTH OF THE UTE.

The current world record for the Dog in a Ute Queue is
699 vehicles. Yes, that's 699 vehicles, parked end to end,
complete with a dog in the flat bed.

NO UTE, NO CIRCLE WORK

THIS CRYPTIC SLOGAN MEANS WHAT IT SAYS: IF YOU DON'T HAVE A UTE,

YOU MAY NOT PARTICIPATE IN THE THRILLING INSANITY OF DRIVING HARD,

FAST AND DUSTY IN CIRCLES IN AN EMPTY PADDOCK IN THE BUSH,

PREFERABLY WITH A HANGOVER.

melbourne miracle

This mysterious smooth, black spread has alternately amused and horrified the rest of the world. Distinctive, unique and suspiciously unrecognisable as a naturally occurring foodstuff, it seems more likely the product of some weird alchemy than a derivative from mother nature. But it blackens the toast of Australians in their millions and has become synonymous with Australiana.

Confused visitors avoid it like the plague. Locals use it with the frequency and familiarity of butter or salt, and it tastes like a magical combination of both.

An accidental by-product of the beer-making process, Vegemite was made from leftover brewer's yeast at the Fred Walker Cheese Company in 1922. It may well have been an oddity, but it was packed with savoury flavour, and the company knew they were on a winner.

A competition was launched to name the product, and one story goes that the winning entry *Vegemite* was supplied by an unknown entrant. However, rumour has it that it was in fact Walker's own seven-year-old daughter who came up with the name on the spot, as she sat with her father while he sorted through the competition entries, attempting to choose a winner.

The following year, the company became the Kraft Walker Cheese Company, and proclaimed Vegemite as one of the world's richest sources of vitamin B.

Generations of migrants have struggled to comprehend the attraction to the piquant spread — Italian and Asian palates assaulted by the lack of subtlety in every bite. Yet a Vegemite lover finds few pleasures as great, starting each day with ritual regularity, daubing or spreading according to individual style, and even packing a jar for travels overseas.

Although Vegemite is no longer Australian-owned, it is still made only in Melbourne. As global culture and cuisine spread themselves across the globe, Vegemite is recast as a daily reminder of the importance of a unique and original Australian cultural fabric. It stands, too, as a reminder of the profound isolation that once quarantined Australia's curios and oddities so completely.

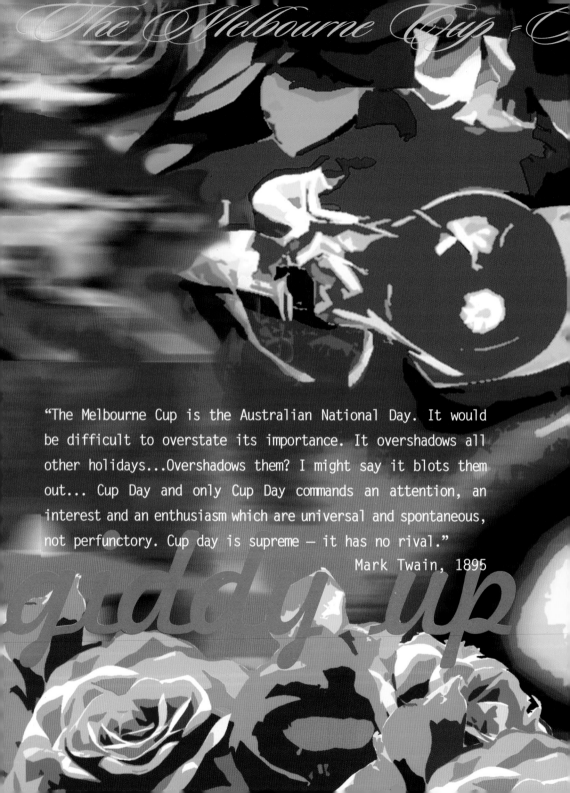

"The Melbourne Cup is the Australian National Day. It would be difficult to overstate its importance. It overshadows all other holidays...Overshadows them? I might say it blots them out... Cup Day and only Cup Day commands an attention, an interest and an enthusiasm which are universal and spontaneous, not perfunctory. Cup day is supreme — it has no rival."

Mark Twain, 1895

giddy up

John Pascoe Fawkner organised Melbourne's first horse race meeting in 1838 on some rough and ready tracks marked out on Batman's Hill (near Spencer Street Station). It was a raucous and drunken affair. Fawkner, who was a publican, had set up his grog shop by the track for the day, and it was well and truly drunk dry.

The race programme offered Races and 'Horse Collar' Grinning Contests (the horse collar framing a funny face competition) on day one. The boozy crowd disported itself in a very rowdy manner and things deteriorated by day two, which saw fallen horses, thrown riders, and the death of a prostitute from Flinders Lane who, for reasons unclear, ran distraught, deranged and directly into the Yarra River, where she drowned.

Things improved the following year, but racing was eventually moved to Flemington in 1840.

After the discovery of gold in Victoria in 1851, gold shipments and horse racing brought the bushrangers out of hiding, in order to survey the very best horses to steal to aid their careers.

Ned Kelly had a legendary love for good horses. Ben Hall is rumoured to have stolen a horse named Troubador no less than nine times. And bushranger Captain Thunderbolt (Fred Ward) started his career as a jockey.

It is rumoured that the dogged, if unsuccessful, Kelly-pursuer Captain Freddie Standish was the one who suggested the Melbourne Cup idea, one grand race to capitalise on what he saw as 'a lot of people come into new money, with little idea of what to do with it'. He thought that a very large prize for one race would be a great lure. He was so right, he should perhaps have been in tourism-marketing instead of law enforcement.

The first Melbourne Cup was held in 1861. The winner, Archer, took a prize of £170 and a gold watch. Today the total prize pool is around $4 million, $2 million for first place.

The Melbourne Cup is now sponsored by and named for breweries, much as things were powered by Fawkner's kegs on the Yarra banks in 1838. The big race day is just as raucous and drunken an affair as Melbourne's first ever race meeting, but it is also now a nationally sanctioned obsession. The whole country watches as 24 horses run a two-mile dash in around three minutes. Unified by horseflesh and the promise of luck, the nation has a $10 million flutter on the Cup. Horseflesh and cash — a bushranger's dream come true.

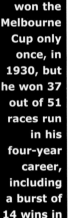

The great Pharlap won the Melbourne Cup only once, in 1930, but he won 37 out of 51 races run in his four-year career, including a burst of 14 wins in a row.

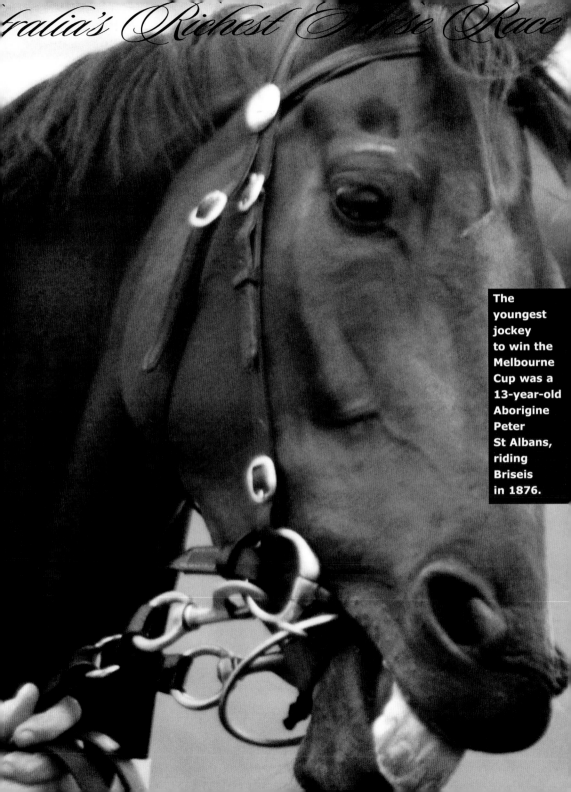

The
youngest
jockey
to win the
Melbourne
Cup was a
13-year-old
Aborigine
Peter
St Albans,
riding
Briseis
in 1876.

The Melbourne Cup

And they're off!:

1861 — Archer	1890 — Carbine	1920 — Poitrel
1862 — Archer	1891 — Malvolio	1921 — Sister Ol.
1863 — Banker	1892 — Glenloth	1922 — King Ingo
1864 — Lantern	1893 — Tarcoola	1923 — Bitalli
1865 — Toryboy	1894 — Patron	1924 — Backwood
1866 — The Barb	1895 — Auraria	1925 — Windbag
1867 — Tim Whiffler	1896 — New Haven	1926 — Spearfelt
1868 — Glencoe	1897 — Gaulus	1927 — Trivalve
1869 — Warrior	1898 — The Grafter	1928 — Statesman
1870 — Nimblefoot	1899 — Merriwee	1929 — Nightmarch
1871 — The Pearl	1900 — Clean Sweep	1930 — Phar Lap
1872 — The Quack	1901 — Revenue	1931 — White Nose
1873 — Don Juan	1902 — The Victory	1932 — Peter Pan
1874 — Haricot	1903 — Lord Cardigan	1933 — Hall Mark
1875 — Wollomai	1904 — Acrasia	1934 — Peter Pan
1876 — Briseis	1905 — Blue Spec	1935 — Marabou
1877 — Chester	1906 — Poseidon	1936 — Wotan
1878 — Calamia	1907 — Apologue	1937 — The Trump
1879 — Darriwell	1908 — Lord Nolan	1938 — Catalogue
1880 — Grand Flaneur	1909 — Prince Foote	1939 — Rivette
1881 — Zulu	1910 — Comedy King	1940 — Old Rowley
1882 — The Assyrian	1911 — The Parisian	1941 — Skipton
1883 — Martini-Henry	1912 — Piastre	1942 — Colonus
1884 — Malua	1913 — Posinatus	1943 — Dark Felt
1885 — Sheet Anchor	1914 — Kingsburgh	1944 — Sirius
1886 — Arsenal	1915 — Patrobas	1945 — Rainbird
1887 — Dunlop	1916 — Sasanof	1946 — Russia
1888 — Mentor	1917 — Westcourt	1947 — Hiraji
1889 — Bravo	1918 — Night Watch	1948 — Rimfire
	1919 — Artilleryman	1949 — Foxzami

Australia's Richest Horse Race

The Lawn, Flemington, (detail)
by Carl Kahler, 1888

950 — Coomic Court
951 — Delta
952 — Dalray
953 — Wodalla
954 — Rising Fast
955 — Toparoa
956 — Evening Peal
957 — Straight Draw
958 — Baystone
959 — MacDougal
960 — Hi Jinx
961 — Lord Fury
962 — Even Stevens
963 — Gatum Gatum
964 — Polo Prince
965 — Light Fingers
966 — Galilee
967 — Red Handed
968 — Rain Lover
969 — Rain Lover
970 — Baghdad Note
971 — Silver Knight
972 — Piping Lane
973 — Gala Supreme
974 — Think Big
975 — Think Big
976 — Van Der Hum
977 — Gold & Black
978 — Arwon
979 — Hyperno

1980 — Beldale Ball
1981 — Just a Dash
1982 — Gurner's Lane
1983 — Kiwi
1984 — Black Knight
1985 — What a Nuisance
1986 — At Talaq
1987 — Kensei
1988 — Empire Rose
1989 — Tawriffic
1990 — Kingston Rule
1991 — Let's Elope
1992 — Subzero
1993 — Vintage Crop
1994 — Jeune
1995 — Doriemus
1996 — Saintly
1997 — Might and Power
1998 — Jezabeel
1999 — Rogan Josh
2000 — Brew
2001 — Ethereal
2002 — Media Puzzle
2003 — Makybe Diva

A Sydney horse won the first two Cups. That was enough to keep them interested in Melbourne's great race day and to guarantee the national status of the event. Had it been hogged from the start by Melbourne winners, who knows if the support would have been as enthusiastic, and national participation so well established from the outset. The other states haven't been able to stay away from the Melbourne Cup ever since.

The Melbourne Cup

OH, JUST PICK A NUMBER...
Of the 24 horses that run the cup, certain numbers it would seem are luckier than others: Horses numbered 4 have won more Melbourne Cups (eleven) than any other number since 1861, while 'unlucky' 13 has actually won twice as many times (four) as 'lucky' 7 (twice).

# of change

Few things can push a city forward with greater momentum than gold. When Victoria's rich gold resources poured out of the ground and into its grand buildings and institutions in the 1850s, Melbourne saw transformation at a speed few other cities in the world have ever enjoyed. Over the following hundred years the more measured advancements, alterations and additions to Melbourne have not caused much stir. Until Crown. Cast as the symbol of radical change in Melbourne, Crown came as a very shiny shock to Melbourne's system.

Gambling venues came much later to Victoria than to other states, and until the introduction of poker machines in 1992, Melburnians looking for gaming action travelled across the border to NSW to play the poker machines, or ventured to Adelaide or Hobart's casinos. Between the advent of Crown's temporary home in the World Trade Centre and the opening of the entertainment complex in 1997 on the Yarra's south bank, Melbourne wrestled with the idea of such a venue. Gambling revenue — the 20th century equivalent of a rich gold seam — poured into an enormous renovation of this long neglected stretch of Yarra riverbank at a scale that had not been seen in Melbourne for over a hundred years.

Great pains were taken by Crown's developers to create a place that would be accepted by Melburnians. Highest standards were set for quality of both construction and presentation of service. But the bedrock of Melbourne's mainstream public opinion has proved a difficult seam to tap, and anti-gaming sentiment remains strong in the city. Although for some, Crown will never be acceptable, for others it is a far superior venue to its Sydney or Las Vegas counterparts. It is in fact the largest gaming venue in the southern hemisphere, attracting 386,000 visitors every week. The riverbank at Crown has been transformed completely. Transformed by scale, by success, and by hourly explosions of gold.

the fortunes
of change

The Yarra River at The Falls began in 1835 as the very heart of Melbourne enterprise. Each year more and more ships crammed their way into the small port, until after just a decade or so, the city outgrew the river's capacity and so moved its business to road, rail and ports apart. After abandoning the wharf area in the 1850s Melbourne's focus shifted to the city centre, and the original wharf and customs area slid into disfavour. The Grand Hotels of the 1880s were all built in the new city grid, while the riverfront was used for a jumble of light industrial purposes, and largely ignored for decades. And Melbourne's central scenic asset, the Yarra River, was overlooked. It was not until the early 1990s that modern eyes appraised the Yarra's banks and saw the marvellous potential waiting there.

The Southbank precinct of 1992 tugged at the centre of balance of Melbourne's CBD for the first time since Hoddle's city grid was laid. The result was the first real challenge to the likes of good-time zones Carlton, Prahran and St Kilda, and the return of focus to the long-neglected riverfront at the very spot where Melbourne began.

Crown added its substantial weight to the area in 1997, generating a whole new centre of activity in Melbourne, and once more changing the fortunes of the riverfront, placing it squarely at the centre of the action.

The Crown Entertainment Complex covers 510,000m^2, over a 500m river frontage — the equivalent of two city blocks.

Crown employs 6500 staff and contains theatres, retail, hotel, restaurants, conference rooms, gaming, cinemas, entertainment arcades and its own staff training college. The sheer scale of Crown's consumption and turnover are staggering. It has been a major phenomenon, creating an impact on Melbourne's history and landscape of immense importance.

A notable by-product of Crown's existence is that it offered young Asian Melburnians a new place to claim as their own — a place separate from the Chinatown of their grandparents' and great-grandparents' generations. It deliberately extended an overt welcome to Asian Australians in order to attract their patronage, a fact that may well prove to have been a significant factor in accelerating their sense of belonging in a more international 21st century Melbourne.

Crown developer Lloyd Williams demanded perfection in all things associated with the construction of this landmark icon. His constant scrutiny became legendary during the construction years, requiring the custom design of most fixtures and fittings; repeated revisions, improvements and replacements of carpets, marble, finishes and furnishings, until even the most minor details were perfect. His exacting standards have ensured the enduring quality of the appearance of Crown, despite years of continuous use by millions of visitors. If Melbourne had to have a casino, this was the one to have.

Crown Towers Hotel room service prepares 90,000 eggs, 40 km of spaghetti and 55 km of noodles each year.

vn houses an art collection
valued at over $7.5 million

32 chandeliers
use 12,720 bulbs
every three years

Crown's launch advertisement 'PROCESSION' avoided Vegas-style casino
glitz and gave Melbourne a stylish pageant extravaganza on film, in
keeping with a city in love with the arts. Made with a huge film crew
of 75 combined with a cast of 90 performers wearing 157 costumes, six
months of production culminating in two weeks of filming and four weeks
of animation, and all to the tune of a 126-piece symphony orchestra, this
masterpiece of staging and high-tech wizardry will pass the test of time
as one of the great feats of the Australian advertising film industry.

chong lim

"For me New York is Gershwin, Sydney is Cold Chisel, and Melbourne will always be a Paul Kelly song. It was the sound of the word 'Melbourne' that always attracted me. 'Sydney' sounded hard. From far-off Malaysia, 'Melbourne' sounded so different to me...like the final foreign frontier.**"**

wowsers

Traditionally Melbourne has rejected a progress-at-any-cost mentality, preferring a more studied progress.

Perhaps it hasn't needed progress at any cost. Melbourne had been made perfect by gold, so what was the rush? Indeed, during the gold boom, every opportunist that could do so made his way to Melbourne to strike it lucky. Drunks, prostitutes and thieves filled the once quiet streets with gambling, drinking and carousing. What a shock for those who'd had marvellous Melbourne all to themselves until then. During the gold and land boom years of the 1860s to 1890s, Melbourne was wild, unregulated, a free-for-all for the brash and the hedonistic. But after the boom came the bust, and a more sober, 'Victorian' approach to community life.

The term *wowser* had been used to describe 'a person who is obnoxious or annoying to the community or who is in some way disruptive', such as a drunk or a prostitute.

But very soon after the term was used to refer to those who were obnoxious or annoying because they *hindered* this looser behaviour, namely those who frowned on drinking and prostitution. And so *wowser* grew to mean: Purist, wet-blanket, finger-wagging do-gooder, altruist, stick in the mud, discourager, abstainer, moralising moaner, soberside, pious prude, party-pooper, killjoy, professional whinger, and pragmatic pulpit-pounding self-absorbed nag.

Melbourne, like any city, has had its fair share of wowsers, who have aimed to curb the vices of Melburnians, from indulging in gambling, alcohol and prostitution, to following leisure pursuits on Sunday, the Christian day of rest. And although 6 o'clock closing in pubs is long a thing of the past, and gambling and prostitution laws have been relaxed, there remains in Melbourne an undercurrent of the ever-watchful eye of the wowser.

Melbourne has avoided the no-holds-barred indulgences of Sydney town, the Buy Now, Pay Later thinking of rapid development. Melbourne's is a more considered advance. Although the Kennett ethos of the late 1990s accelerated Melbourne's lurch forward via development and privatisation, it is the exception that proves the rule. Hopefully the surges in progress that do occur are all the better in quality for the pressure of such regular and rigorous scrutiny.

Melbourne loves a party, preferably an arty party, and preferably with a parade. Each year the city celebrates Moomba in March, the Melbourne Fashion Festival also in March, the Comedy Festival in April, the Melbourne International Film Festival in July, the *Age* Melbourne Writer's Festival in August, the Melbourne Fringe Festival in September, the Melbourne Festival in October, the AFL Grand Final Parade in October, the Melbourne Cup in November... any and every excuse for the year's creativity to burst onto stage, screen, or street. It's a measure of the continuing increases in the city's population size, mix and sophistication that Melbourne can support so much festival activity. But in the beginning it was just Moomba, once the One-and-Only street party. Born in the family-oriented 50s, Moomba is Melbourne's original festival. At its peak, all of Melbourne loved just one parade, and one parade said it all. After 50 years, it is regularly outshone by bigger, slicker parades. But despite being considered old-fashioned and unsophisticated, Moomba rumbles on. Renamed the Moomba Waterfest in 2002, it is striving to reinvent itself, now linking its identity more strongly with a celebration of the Yarra River.

moomba

moomba

Two boomerangs — inverted, a clown's collar skirt and a cone hat, a naive smile and a trusting leap from a bass drum festooned with chains. The Moomba man is the original Melbourne icon. Daggy, parochial, corny, this little figure seems to represent all the disarmingly un-sophisticated, cardigan-honest things that only Melbourne can be. A city that had a family feel and a suburban mentality. Like the 1956 Olympics, Moomba was made in less mercenary, more meaningful times.

In 1955, Moomba began as a street spectacular. Meaning 'let's get together and have fun' Moomba was held for the last 10 days of summer. The party culminated on the Monday Labour Day holiday. Floats decked out with exotic figures and gaudy displays would rumble down Swanston Street where the whole city would turn out for a day of Melbourne pride.

We celebrated local creations, not international ones, encouraging Melbourne's own stars like Graham Kennedy, Bert Newton, The Seekers, Zig and Zag, and Princess Panda. We turned out in support of our local industries, TV, retail, and manufacturing, and applauded local efforts in agriculture and business. We were knitting an identity that belonged to Melbourne only. We were celebrating our own efforts. It was unsophisticated but comforting, even edifying.

Fifty years on, Moomba's now outdated format limps forward on a much smaller scale — an open air art show, free concerts at the Myer Music Bowl, the flying Birdman competition, water-skiing on the Yarra, the obligatory fireworks finale.

But the cringe culture of the 1970s and 80s has seen Moomba abandoned in favour of a more international style entertainment. Bigger, glossier, corporate-backed festivals have pushed Moomba aside — literally, with the lately acquired Grand Prix competing for the very same weekend since 1997.

But despite a lack of funds and fashionability, the festival is enjoyed by Melbourne's ethnic groups, who use it well as a display of culture and unity.

Without major sponsorship Moomba may be pushed aside altogether. Perhaps it needs a heritage listing to protect it, as a much-loved part of Melbourne's emotional landscape. On the other hand, now the cultural cringe has well and truly been vapourised by an explosion of Melbourne-born confidence and talent around the world, with new thinking and new funding Moomba may well rise phoenix-like to once again become the showcase of all that is Melbourne's own and Melbourne's best.

PRINCESS PANDA: CELEBRITY 60S-STYLE

TONIGHT-SHOW'S KING KENNEDY'S DRIVEABLE DESK EXPLODES MID-PARADE

MOOMBA TROPHY AWARDED TO LEONARD MONCUR, FILM MAKER AND WINNER OF
THE ANNUAL MOOMBA 8MM MOVIE CLUB COMPETITION, AMATEUR STATUS 1962.

graham

" Admit it...you've heard that my unspectacular love life has been the despair of the TV gossip columnists. Well it's my turn to make an admission: I've been conducting a secret and very satisfying love affair for years...It's with my one and only love: that haughty dignified dame — Melbourne. **"**

Graham Kennedy 1967

kennedy

the king

Graham Kennedy. King of Melbourne Television. Compere of *In Melbourne Tonight*, Australia's formative live variety show, Kennedy was a legend in our lounge rooms five nights a week for 12 years. Australia's first and most successful tonight show host, Kennedy invented Australian TV style — direct, irreverent and unpredictable. While Australia was still dazzled by TV itself and by the fake frenzy of US game shows, Kennedy's style was relaxed, confident, underwhelmed. With his dry wit and double entendre, he was a master of laconic mischief.

Kennedy played with the medium and parodied the format. With neither American accent nor British plum, he leapfrogged over the Aussie cultural cringe even before we knew we had one. He was a natural comedian. His physical antics were slapstick-hysterical, his timing perfect. But his ace was his understanding of the new medium; the intimacy of TV. He seduced the camera, spoke quietly, drew us in close, made us part of his mischief and then exploded with laughter at his own jokes. His clean-cut but funny-face looks were the perfect launching place for irreverence. His sharp-toothed grin put the devil into even the straightest lines.

Practical jokes and advertising blurred into a running gag that left audiences in stitches for over a decade. He broke every rule he could, rethought every 'given' notion, rejected and reinvented it. Kennedy's desk was even motorised so he could drive it around the set. He eventually drove it down Swanston Street in the Moomba parade. Via sketch comedy and live advertising segments (one famed to have continued for over 20 minutes) his delivery was unpredictable and uncontrollable, which made for dangerous and extremely funny live TV. In fact, during the second incarnation of his show in 1975, Kennedy let loose the 'F' word, on live television, disguising it as a mock crow's cry: 'Faaaaark! Faaaaark!'.

He didn't last long after that. His show was censored by order of network chairman Kerry Packer. His jokes were vetted and his previously Live shows pre-taped and edited, until he finally quit the show later the same year. Kennedy eventually went on to host game shows and then beyond TV to movies. In his later years he retired from the public scene altogether, remaining a recluse to this day at his bush retreat home.

Although others have outlasted him in front of the camera, not a single one comes close to the magic that was Graham Kennedy Live. Alone in the frontierland of live transmission, he adlibbed his way through the very birth of Australian TV. The pale and cheeky boy from St Kilda remains the best there ever was.

Graham Kennedy illustrates the difference between mere success and stardom. He may well have left the screen long ago but his position is unassailable in history as the undisputed King of Australian TV.

NAUGHTY AND NICE. GRAHAM KENNEDY WON 10 LOGIE AWARDS, HIS SHOW WON FIVE, BUT HE NEVER HOSTED THE LOGIES NIGHT ITSELF. FAR TOO IRREVERENT AND HARD TO CORRAL, HIS SHARP WIT WAS AHEAD OF HIS TIME, ALTHOUGH HIS DELIVERY WOULD RIVAL THAT OF ANY OSCARS HOST OF TODAY. BERT NEWTON, HOWEVER, WAS THE CONSUMMATE LOGIES HOST – DIPLOMATIC, SUAVE, NEVER A WORD OUT OF PLACE, ALWAYS NAUGHTY ENOUGH TO GUARANTEE A GOOD NIGHT BUT NEVER UNKIND. BERT JUST GOT BETTER AND BETTER UNTIL HE BECAME THE MASTER OF THE MASTERS OF CEREMONIES, HOSTING THE LOGIES SHOW 18 TIMES.

made in melbourne

Melbourne was always the true engine of Australian-made television. TV arrived in Australia's lounge rooms in 1956, transmitted from a handful of regional stations, each limited by technology to broadcasting to its own local territory. Melbourne viewers took up the new craze faster than any other city, leading the nation in household TV ownership for years. Although in Melbourne HSV7 was technically first off the mark in July, GTV9 took off six months later and then took control with *In Melbourne Tonight* (IMT) in May 1957.

IMT, a live nightly variety show hosted by a 23-year-old Graham Kennedy, defined Melbourne TV from then on. GTV9 soon lured rival HSV7 host Bert Newton to its team and gained a reputation as the most powerful creative stable right from the beginning.

In 1960 with the advent of coaxial cable came the ability to broadcast nationally, and the inevitable merger of regional stations into larger groups. Although ATN7 in Sydney had been GTV9 Melbourne's affiliate for some time, it was Sydney's TCN9 and Melbourne's GTV9 that merged to become one in 1960. And it was Melbourne's GTV9 that retained the lead in production status for some time to come from its headquarters in an ex-Heinz factory in Richmond.

IMT was now broadcast beyond Melbourne to a national audience under the new name of *The Graham Kennedy Show*. Its sketch format launched the great personalities of the industry, most still going strong today after nearly 50 years.

This was as close as we got to our own Hollywood Rat Pack — the backbone of Australian TV: Graham Kennedy, Bert Newton, Philip Brady, Joff Ellen and announcers Pete Smith and later Bruce Mansfield. Stovepipe suits, narrow ties, pointy shoes, puns and innuendo all combined with a sophisticated new medium to make stars out of Melbourne boys. And girls. IMT presented the world's first ever female tonight show host in Toni Lamond, among an assortment of dozens of guest-hosts that supported Kennedy. Eventually it closed in 1969 after 3000 appearances by Kennedy over 12 years.

Melbourne continued to generate great national TV. Kennedy was followed by the *Don Lane Show* for eight years, teaming Don Lane with Bert Newton. Melbourne's GTV9 also produced an unbeatable 28 years of Darryl Somer's *Hey Hey It's Saturday*, the live broadcasting phenomenon of the 1970s.

The ABC's *Countdown* was another Melbourne TV production success, delivering a Sunday night TV hit parade every week for 13 years from 1974 to 1987. Hosted by Ian 'Molly' Meldrum, the unlikely compere viewers loved to rubbish for his stumbling commentaries, *Countdown* became a national touchstone and an international force to be acknowledged, as indeed did Meldrum himself.

Maybe it was the TV-friendly climate, maybe it was the talent pool, but from the beginning, Melbourne preferred to make its own fun rather than watch imported shows. That investment in creative talent and production expertise is still the basis of the best of Australian TV style: spontaneous, unpredictable, authentic family fun.

IMT HAD THE FIRST FEMALE HOST (TONI LAMOND) ON A TONIGHT SHOW ANYWHERE IN THE WORLD.
IMT HAD THE FIRST WHEEL ON A TONIGHT SHOW ANYWHERE IN THE WORLD.

co'mpére:(-par)
1.*n*., [F,=godfather, f.Rom. *compater* (as COM-, L *pater* father, with the father)]

GRAHAM AND PHILIP BRADY

1956
Australian TV begins

1957
IMT launches Kennedy, Newton, Brady *et al*.

1958
The Logies begin, with Kennedy and Panda as the first winners

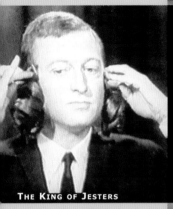

THE KING OF JESTERS

IN 1958, SYDNEY'S TOP TEN SHOWS WERE ALL US IMPORTS — FIVE WESTERNS, FOUR SITCOMS AND DISNEYLAND. IN MELBOURNE, GRAHAM KENNEDY'S RATINGS GREW TO A 50% SHARE OF VIEWERS, FIVE NIGHTS A WEEK. AS A CULTURAL TOUCHSTONE, IMT WAS UNPARALLELED. IT CONNECTED MELBURNIANS IN THE IMMEDIATE WAY THAT TV ALONE CAN DO, AND WITH A NIGHTLY DOSE OF FUN AND IRREVERENCE, THE CITY AND THE MEDIUM GREW UP TOGETHER.

COUNTDOWN HOST IAN 'MOLLY' MELDRUM

TV OWNERSHIP

956 : Melb 5%	Sydney 1%	
957 : Melb 26%	Sydney 12%	
958 : Melb 46%	Sydney 41%	
959 : Melb 63%	Sydney 59%	
960 : Melb 76%	Sydney 71%	
961 : Melb 78%	Sydney 79%	
962 : Melb 82%	Sydney 82%	
963 : Melb 83%	Sydney 86%	
964 : Melb 90%	Sydney 88%	
965 : Melb 91%	Sydney 90%	

969 TV ownership at 81% of all ralian households nationwide.

BERT, GRAHAM AND JOFF ELLEN, 1961

1960
Coaxial cable allows national transmission

1971-99
Hey Hey It's Saturday
has a 28-year run

1974-87
13 years of ABC's *Countdown*

AND BARREL GIRL PANDA, 1960

'TELEVISION BEGAN

FIRST IN SYDNEY,

BUT BEST IN

MELBOURNE.'

GERALD STONE, *COMPULSIVE VIEWING* 2001

PHILIP BRADY, PATTI AND BERT NEWTON

MELBOURNE WILL BE FINE, OVERCAST, LATE SHOWER

MILD, SCATTERED CLOUD, WARM, CLEAR, SUNN

SEABREEZES, WINDS FRESHENING, BROKEN CLOU

MODERATE NW WIND, CLOUD INCREASING, LIGHT RAI

THUNDERSTORMS, HAZE, SUNNY BREAKS, MOSTLY CLOUD

RAIN DEVELOPING, SOME FLOODING, OVERNIGHT DRIZZL

WARM TO HOT, LIGHT WIND, MORNING FOG, HEAVY RAI

WINDS GUSTING, CLOUDY PERIODS, GALE WARNIN

SMOKE FROM BUSHFIRES, CLOUDLESS, FRESH GUSTY S

WINDS CONTRACTING TO THE SW, SQUALLS, HIGH CLOUD

HAZY AT TIMES, STRONG SE WIND, HOT TO EXTREMELY HO

HAILSTORMS, FREQUENT SHOWERS, PATCHY RAI

ISOLATED SHOWERS, SUNNY PERIODS, RELATIVE HUMIDIT

SMOG, HOT NORTHERLY WINDS, RAIN OVERNIGH

POSSIBLE STORMS, MOSTLY SUNNY, SNOW ON OR ABOU

THE RANGES, LOW CLOUD, FOG, UV RADIATION, MAINL

CLOUDY, RAIN CLEARING OVERNIGHT AND BECOMING FINE

If you don't
like the weather
in Melbourne,
wait a minute

weather/or/not

Meteorologically, Melbourne is on an emotional rollercoaster. Where else can you get such variety of weather, such natural beauty? Where can you get an environmental mood swing so grey that it can stop you in your tracks and compel you to reflect? Or one so unexpected and blithely uplifting it can inspire you to do something equally as unlikely?

Solid Victorian bluestone stands impervious in hot, dry northerly winds one minute; rain squalls send you scurrying home to soup the next. Tropical palms disappear into fog, and once a year God drops a bag of crisps under every tree overnight and calls it Autumn. Melbourne paints pictures with incongruous combinations of landscape and light. You can walk to work in a watercolour, and wade home waist deep in oils.

How do people in less capricious climes get a truly meaty, thunderous blue mood going without a Melbourne downpour to really set the scene, and vindicate their feelings with a backing track of lightning and thunder? How can you be truly rebellious or even merely pensive in the constant saccharine sunshine of a locale that's perfect one day and perfect the next? And who can stay angry on a clear Melbourne autumn day?

This city has its own personality, its own good and bad hair days. Never bland, always different.

In Melbourne we live amid constant proof that tomorrow's another day. No matter what may happen today, there's bound to be something totally new around the corner. Always another chance. It's quite therapeutic, and teaches us to be hopeful, optimistic, adaptable, pragmatic, tolerant, flexible, spontaneous and innovative. You can't plan as easily, you can't control as readily. And that's got to be good for your soul. No wonder it's a city for artists.

The lowest
temperature
on record in
Australia
was −23°
recorded in
NSW in
June 1994

If a change is
as good as a
holiday, then
Melbourne's
a world tour

Melbourne's
highest recorded
temperature is
49.4°, recorded
in January 1906

Melbourne's
average
maximum
summer
temperature
is 24°C
...the same
as Sydney's

weather/or/not

Melbourne's average annual rainfall is less than half that of Sydney

Four seasons in one day

Melbourne's average annual rainfall is 400 mm in west Melbourne, and 600 mm in east Melbourne, compared to Sydney's annual average of 1200 mm

In February 2002, Melbourne experienced the highest number of days of electrical thunderstorms on record for summer

weather/or/not

'Melbourne's temperature range is more conducive to reading than sunbaking — which contributes to its intellect more than in Sydney, where the sun beats down and turns people into lizards that lay basking. I always enjoyed Melbourne's winter. It increased my reading exponentially.' PHILLIP ADAMS

love, me

bea

MELBOURNE

OPPORTUNITY | SANCTUARY | PASSION | BEAUTY

uty

helena rubinstein | fashion | le louvre | the seat of
good design | architecture CBD | banks | theatres |
flinders street station | sculpture | sculpture finder

effie
actor mary coustas

" Melbourne in a word? 'Grouse.' Melbourne is a Star Factory. It's got the three Cs: Coffee, Culcha and did I mention Coffee? I'm big on the environment, that's why I love Melbourne — except for the elements — there's just too many variables for a woman as hair proud as myself. I've got hair products for every season. In fact, Melbourne is like hairspray. You can barely notice it, you know? But everything is in place, just perfect. And the more you get used to it, the harder it is to go without it. **"**

helena rubir

(1870-1965)

Helena Rubinstein was a Polish immigrant who arrived in Australia at the age of 18 in 1888. She noticed the ruddy complexions of Melbourne's women, caused by exposure to the unpredictable Melbourne climate. Her opportunity lay literally in the face of adversity, and Melbourne's famous weather inspired Rubinstein to create an international beauty empire.

Although her stay in Melbourne was a short one, it was in Melbourne that Helena Rubinstein found her life's work and launched herself on the path to international success. In six short years in Melbourne, she began the business that would take her name to the world.

After her arrival in Australia, Rubinstein worked for her uncle in his grocery at Coleraine in Victoria's Western District. After 8 years she moved to Melbourne town. There, she noticed the ruddy complexions of colonial women, caused by Melbourne's hot/dry/cold/wet climate. She had studied medicine in Switzerland for a short time, and so had both the means and the resolve to do something about it.

> 'Creation must be bold. it must surpass what has been done before.' H.R.

She developed her famous 'crème Valaze' and opened a small shop in Melbourne in 1902. She advised women individually on customised treatment regimes for their skin, and pioneered the idea of individual skin consultation and the use of a skin treatment routine, which are now so commonplace.

After just six years of business in Melbourne, Rubinstein left for England in 1908 with the equivalent of US$100,000 to expand her business. She never returned, and the rest is history.

At the age of 38 she married an American journalist in England and had two sons. She lived in Paris until the war years, when she moved to the USA. In 1937, she divorced and at 68 married Prince Artchil Gourielli-Tchkonia, a man 20 years her junior.

> 'It seems to me impossible to work in the beauty business with out being a passionate art lover.' H.R.

Her ultimate success brought immense wealth. Rubinstein, like her Melbourne contemporaries, was a generous philanthropist. She inaugurated the Helena Rubinstein Art Scholarship, won by the likes of Charles Blackman in 1960, Fred Williams in 1963 and Jan Senbergs in 1966. She also established the Helena Rubinstein Science prize, Helena Rubinstein Pavilion of Contemporary Art, and the Helena Rubinstein Foundation, which funded many other philanthropic ventures. Rubinstein remained active in business, art and society until her death at 95.

ke Sidney Myer, Rubinstein was both extremely wealthy and extremely generous. The business aders of the 19th and early 20th centuries had strong social consciences and their nerous philanthropy is in striking contrast with the corporate raids, takeovers and rorts at have so far defined many corporate leaders of the late 20th and 21st centuries.

even

eathcote

66 It's a style over substance thing. I've danced at the Sydney Opera House — it's externally an exquisite building but backstage? Beautiful form, but as for function...The Melbourne State Theatre on the other hand, is modest, even unremarkable to look at by comparison. But once inside, it has such a rich atmosphere, such comfort, and a sort of surrounding soul. Melbourne's a bit like that. 99

FAS

FASHION
melbourne means

257

FASHION

"Melbourne fashion is intelligent fashion... Never flash trash."

Jenny Bannister, designer

JENNY BANNISTER DESIGN, 2002 MELBOURNE FASHION FESTIVAL

FASHION

Melbourne is the undisputed fashion capital of Australia. The history of it is Melbourne's thriving drapery, millinery and tailoring businesses, begun by European migrants and boosted by the gold wealth of the 1850s. Flinders Lane became the very heart of Australian fashion importing, manufacture and retailing, and is still home today to businesses established before Federation.

Melbourne's climate is more European, allowing similarly 'continental' expressions of fashion. Hats, gloves, umbrellas, boots, waistcoats, vests, scarves, overcoats and sunglasses...Melbourne enjoys an arsenal of accessories, all the paraphernalia of style. The ever-changing climate demands a flexible and creative attitude to both outings and wardrobes. This allows legitimate indulgence in the extremes of fashion, a great variety worn in the course of just one season, one month, and often in just one week.

Then of course there's Melbourne style. A boob tube will get you by in Sydney, in Queensland shorts and a singlet cover most bods, and in Far North Queensland a sarong and thongs will suffice. But in Melbourne, there are standards. All the trappings of establishment fashion find endless expression in Melbourne, which gives Melburnians a more complex demeanour than the casual, dressed-down states. Assumptions about books and covers notwithstanding, Melbourne style is simply more credible.

With more need for interseasonal wardrobes, more variety in the ranges offered, wider fabric selection and more garments on the go, there's more to make, more to need, more to wear, more reason to buy. More experience, more experimentation, more understanding. Which all makes Melbourne the much better-dressed metropolis.

RACIN

milasch

Lager

é lau

MELBOURNE'S FASHION SUPREMACY

has its roots in some quite definite surges of fashion passion.

More than anywhere else in the rest of colonial Australia, Melbourne's gold rush boom of the 1850s tipped the population mix completely, swamping the dour, unfashionable squattocracy with fortune-hunting foreigners. Just 15 years after settlement, hundreds of thousands of migrants, mostly Europeans, flooded through Melbourne. Of those who struck it rich many stayed and re-created a continental lifestyle for themselves, augmented by the best that money could buy, including fashion. They needed bustles, brocades, brogues, and beautiful places to be seen. Many of those who were unlucky on the goldfields also stayed and plied their trade as tailors, milliners and cobblers or as importers exploiting their connections back home, bringing Europe's best to the hungry nouveau riche. Still others opened cafés, restaurants, and theatres, creating the essential addresses of a fashionable society.

Melbourne's post-WWII period saw a second surge of Europeans, who would eventually bend the buttoned-up British twinset mentality of the 1950s towards exotica like Italian shoes and ocelot prints. In the three decades after the war, the British population of Melbourne doubled with the migration surge. But the European population increase was a much more noticeable 14-fold, to 11.6 per cent of the state's population. There were more craftsmen, factory workers, seamstresses, piece-workers and importers to add to an already burgeoning

The Lawn, Flemington (detail) by Carl Kahler 1888 La Trobe Collection, State Library of Victoria

ragtrade. The passion was to produce fashions every bit as good as the international standard. The focus was on emulation and excellence in production. The local wool industry enjoyed the establishment of many fine mills in Melbourne, producing high quality knits and woven fabrics, constantly improving the techniques and expertise of the local industry.

Yet another of Melbourne's fashionable passions has been retail. Famous stores like Myer and Georges, and retailing families like the Besens and Gandels of Sussans and Chadstone fame, Blooms of Portmans, Lews of Witchery and Bardas of Sportsgirl, all kept the ragtrade healthy, with busy outlets ready to dispatch locally made product to Melburnians with great style and efficiency. The great stores of Melbourne held immense power within the fashion industry, driving style and direction by dint of their size and control over the ever-loyal customer.

Through the 1960s and 70s, international trends thrived in Melbourne. London's sloan rangers, American preppies and Britain's punks — Melbourne had local versions of them all. In Shoppe, Merivale and Mr John, JAG and other bohemian boutiques kept Melbourne's fashion victims well-dressed in bellbottoms and satin. But it wasn't until the post-punk 1980s that Melbourne began to assert a new kind of love affair with fashion, this time through controlling its own fashion identity.

By the early 1980s, Melbourne was beginning to breed its own unique crop of designers. A fringe event called 'Fashion 82' inspired three Melburnian fringe-dwelling fashionistas to join together and galvanise the design side of the fashion industry. They were fashion's bravest from the 80s avant-garde: graphic artist and radio presenter Robert Pearce; artist and jewellery designer Kate Durham; and 22-year-old Arts/Law graduate Robert Buckingham. All three thrived at the junction of art and fashion, and were inspired by 'Fashion 82' to document on film the 'Fashion 83' event.

Held at St Kilda's 'The Venue' Seaview Ballroom, 'Fashion 83' included young designers Jenny Bannister, Bruce Slorach (later Mambo) & Sara Thorn, Anthony Smedhurst, Rosalind Piggot, Inars Lacis, Clarence Chai, Desbina Collins and Maria Kosic. Attendees included Richard Neville and unpaid models included the likes of Alannah Hill and Deborah Thomas.

Having filmed their documentary, the three soon realised they had stumbled onto a bigger project. They had identified a need in the fledgling fashion design industry for leadership, direction and financial support, and so resolved in 1984 to form the Fashion Design Council (FDC) of Australia to promote and encourage young designers.

For the next six years the FDC ran the yearly 'Fashion' event. They had enlisted a major sponsor, Nescafe by 'Fashion 86'. They established a board of commissioners to run things, including at times writer Lee Tulloch and designer Jenny Bannister. And in 1989 they opened the FDC retail shop, selling young designers' product in the basement of what was once the *Merivale and Mr John* Collins Street store.

But with the death later in 1989 of founding style-guru Robert Pearce, the trio was broken. Kate Durham had her own creative endeavours to pursue, and many of the young designer flock had already begun to stand on their own two retail feet. The FDC was active, mainly as a shop, for a few more years until its close in 1992. Individual designers were detached from the training wheels of the FDC and left to their own devices.

In 1996, the third founding member of the FDC, Robert Buckingham, began as director of the first Melbourne Fashion Festival. Since then the festival has rapidly become Australia's pre-eminent style event, staging two solid weeks of parades, seminars, parties and exhibitions each year.

The Melbourne Fashion Festival now showcases the work of over 250 designers for an audience of 120,000, boosts the Australian GDP by $50 million and channels $25 million in publicity alone. Melbourne's 150 years of experience with fashion importing, manufacture, innovation, design, retailing, marketing and promotion are evidenced in its continuing leadership status in the industry, and in the drop-dead-gorgeous citizens.

"Fashion to my way of thinking is about sending messages out to people, it's about codes, a coded communication about ourselves. The messages Melbourne sends are very much about design, the clothing is style-oriented, rather than in other cities where it's going to be more about a body culture. In Melbourne, the essence we are expressing is less about the outdoors, and more of an internal thing, and in an internal space, clothing and the way one behaves become more important. Melbourne fashion is like Collins Street — at the high end of aspiration, fitted in at the top of a formal city grid, the road made wide and elegant with trees but nonetheless part of that more structured city because of the grid. Melbourne was always a very planned city, so therefore, in a fashion sense that goes through to the structure of clothing, the jacket, the direction, rather than the looseness, the disjointedness you find elsewhere, and that creates that degree of Melbourne style."

Robert Buckingham, Director, Melbourne Fashion Festival

LILLIAN WIGHTMAN (1902–1992). Also known as Diamond Lil, Luxury Lil, The Grande Dame, The Queen of Melbourne fashion, The Doyenne of Fashionable Society, The beguiling Queen of Style, the Doge of Australian Haute Couture.

Lillian Wightman made an icon out of nothing. From thin air she invented Le Louvre, a chiffon palace that became the temple of Australian fashion, and lives on today, at the 'Paris end of Collins Street'.

Lillian would tell you she coined that phrase. And why doubt it? She certainly created the very soul of Melbourne's elite fashion identity, single handed.

In 1922 she came to Melbourne from the bush near Ballarat to be fitted for a bridesmaid's dress. The couturier she visited offered her a job, so she stayed on to learn the techniques of designing and dressmaking. She also learned the techniques of business, and of befriending all the 'leading ladies' of the day.

In 1925, her father lent her £100 to get started on her own. She bought a sewing machine, and set herself up making handkerchief-hem, drop-waisted chiffon frocks for Melbourne's young gels to go dancing in. In those days, Lillian's business was a fashion oasis in a desert far from Europe, and the well-financed flappers were eager for her diaphanous creations. They stuck by her, and eventually became the important ladies of the 1950s and 60s. A few live on as Le Louvre customers today, ever loyal to Lillian's style and charm.

In the early 1920s Lillian married George Weir, a cattle dealer whose dreams of farming the Australian bush didn't mesh well with Lillian's own more elegant plan. She retained her name at marriage, and remained Miss Lillian Wightman always. But despite attempts to make the bush more palatable and transforming the family home into a French provincial bungalow, she knew the country life was not for her. 'Being buried alive in the great Australian loneliness is not for me!' she scoffed. 'Darling, the blowflies up there play like jazz bands on the window sill!' Melbourne and Le Louvre were to remain her focus, and she eventually abandoned the farm for a city home.

'In those days,
women were women,
and I dressed them
and somebody else
undressed them'

MISS LILLIAN WIGHTMAN

'Oh, I couldn't tell you the
chiffon dresses I made.
We simply ate chiffon, hundreds
and hundreds of yards of it.
You just weren't done unless you
were wearing chiffon.
Kissing the body, dear.'

MISS LILLIAN WIGHTMAN

Le Louvre

Lillian opened her 'salon' around 1930, in an unorthodox location — the top of Collins Street — among professional suites and doctors rooms. In a masterstroke of positioning, she stood apart in both location and attitude, and became the darling of the wealthy doctors' wives.

Lillian read all she could about the highlights of Paris society and fashion in the 1920s and 30s. With magazines and books she fed her imagination, and although she had never travelled further than Ballarat, she brought to life a French confection that she called Le Louvre.

For wealthy but isolated Australian ladies of the 1930s, Le Louvre was a branch office of Paris, connecting them to all the finery and culture Melbourne ached for.

Le Louvre specialised in French designer imports and local adaptations created on the premises. Matching her clientele to her French collection, Lillian dressed the cream of Melbourne society in Europe's best.

But there was so much more to Le Louvre than fabulous clothes. 'This is no shop, my dear,' she'd declare. 'This is a salon, a club.' And indeed, no garments obscured the windows, no stock cluttered the interior, and no mention was ever made of accounts.

This was the female equivalent of the Melbourne Club. A place where Lillian and her clients could live out their dreams of civilised society doing fashionable things in a gracious manner. A private circle of ladies sat, with tea cups on their pressed-together knees, gossip on their lips, and cash in their husbands' bank accounts.

'The salon was always a great meeting place, and the discreet gossip was sacred to us all' said Lillian. And no outsider was permitted to intrude into this elite confessional.

Dame Nellie Melba was among the first customers in the 1930s. 'She was very difficult, quite fascinating, and after a *lot* of fuss, she bought a white ermine jacket.'

Lillian had a story about every notable Melburnian and important visitor to Melbourne, and if she didn't have one, she made one up. Miss Wightman and her salon were *the* destination. Governor's ladies, high society Dames, visiting dignitaries, movie stars, artists, models and celebrities... Le Louvre attracted them all. Every name of note in Australia shopped at Le Louvre, many shopping nowhere else. Myer, Melba, Baillieu, Brooks...even Dame Edna Everage chose Lillian's ocelot raincoat. Of the A-list dressing room gossip she often bragged 'I could write a book, but no-one would ever dare publish it!'

Lillian collaborated with the great

ER, MELBA, BAILLIEU, BROOKS...
IS WAS THE FEMALE EQUIVALENT
THE MELBOURNE CLUB.

"I could write a book, but no-one would ever dare publish it!"

Austrian–Australian artist Louis Kahan, a partnership of fashion and illustration which led them to design together for opera and theatre in the 1940s and 50s. Kahan designed Le Louvre's logo and produced many a portrait of his close friend through these years. In turn, Lillian connected Kahan to her inner circle of famous, highly sketchable faces.

In the 1950s, Lillian refurbished the shop, lining the salon with mirrors floor to ceiling, and extending the trompe l'oeil that was Le Louvre. Like the Tardis, this tiny salon seems expansive once inside. Lillian adopted her signature ocelot print after Dior's range featuring ocelot was launched in the 1950s. She used it liberally in her interior design as well as in fashions.

Sidney Myer was so taken by the gilded, glittering salon Lillian had created, he offered her a position in his Bourke Street store running the chandelier department. Although tempted, she took the offer as encouragement only, and stuck to her own enterprise.

Today's Le Louvre is just as special as it ever was, if only just a little more accessible to just a few more Melburnians. The exterior is still aloof and intriguing. Le Louvre does little to explain itself to the passer-by, and is too intimidating for most. A shroud of mysterious tulle is all it takes to deter the faint-hearted from daring to enter.

With an appropriate sense of occasion, the formidable Miss Lillian Wightman died on Melbourne Cup Day 1992 aged 90. So ended a lifetime of courage and creativity, in a town that offered her simple opportunity. Over 600 letters of condolence poured in, from millionaires who were her customers, to the taxi drivers she shared a cold chop with while travelling home. She was influential, forthright, charming and disarmingly down to earth. 'I'm not interested in being buried,' she said. 'When I go, I want to float away like an autumn leaf down Collins Street.'

Now Lillian's daughter Georgina Weir continues the tradition of impeccable service to the very fussiest of customers. With 'only Georges to compete with' Lillian and Georgina had a hands-down winner in the eyes of their exclusive clientele. Georgina now dresses the new daughters of society, delivering hand-picked designs home from Europe, usually with a certain Melbourne socialite in mind.

Lillian Wightman placed a landmark into the business end of Melbourne's story. It's one of the few put there by women. One of the few to last so long. One of the few to touch nearly every big name in Melbourne society, and to do so continuously for nearly 80 years.

the seat of good design

Designed in 1951 by Melbourne's Grant Featherston,the Contour range of Chairs are th
epitome of 1950s chic. After months of musing on how to create a lightweight, flexibl
chair, inspiration for their construction ignited in Featherston's mind one morning a
he rode to work on a Melbourne tram. While fiddling with his tram ticket,tearing an
bending it absentmindedly,Featherston solved a riddle of contour and form with th
tiny scrap of paper. After experimenting further with the same idea in plywood th
Contour range was born, eventually including over 25 different chair designs, featurin
the famous Cone Chair. Embraced by the avant-garde of architecture and design of th
1950s, the chairs became an icon of contemporary style, and 50 years later they remai
at the forefront of modern design as coveted items in the most stylish modern interiors

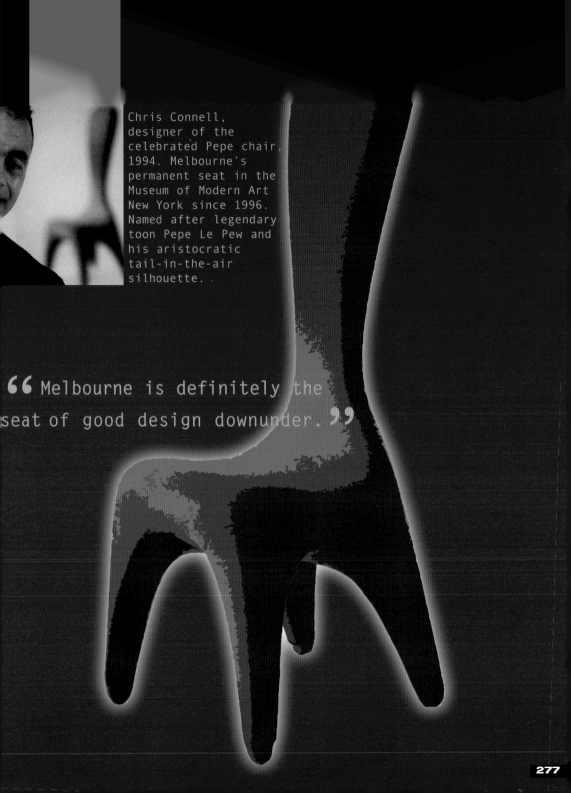

Chris Connell,
designer of the
celebrated Pepe chair,
1994. Melbourne's
permanent seat in the
Museum of Modern Art
New York since 1996.
Named after legendary
toon Pepe Le Pew and
his aristocratic
tail-in-the-air
silhouette.

" Melbourne is definitely the seat of good design downunder. "

As home to the great gold boom buildings of the 1850s onward, the inner city grid contains an extensive collection of architectural styles, including some of the finest examples of their type in the world. Architect William Pitt built a marvellous Melbourne career resulting in the **Olderfleet Building**, the **Princess Theatre**, and the **Melbourne Stock Exchange**. Architects Reed and Barnes gave us the **Exhibition Building** and the **Melbourne Town Hall**, and Charles Webb contributed The **Windsor Hotel** and **Royal Arcade**. The **State Library** opened in 1856, adding a dome over the Reading Room in 1911 that was the largest concrete dome in the world. **Myer's Bourke Street Emporium** was the second largest department store in the world when it was built in 1914, styled on the great Emporium of San Francisco. And Melbourne's Moorish fantasy of 1928, **the Forum Theatre**, was the largest 'picture palace' ever built in Australia. The **Capitol Theatre** of 1925 designed by Walter Burley-Griffin boasts an exquisitely intricate interior that is nothing short of a masterpiece. The iconic **Manchester Unity Building** (opposite) designed in 1929 by Marcus Barlow was built in 1932 for the Independent Order of Oddfellows (IOOF). This 12-storey art deco masterpiece features elaborate interior decoration, and Melbourne's first roof garden café, complete with palms, a lily pond and an aviary of rare and exotic birds. From the 'French-influenced Gothic-revival norman-romanesque' **Magistrate's Court** of 1911, to the 'symmetrically formal neo-Grec beaux-arts-inspired modern French-renaissance style' **Spencer Street Mail Exchange** of 1917, Melbourne has collected a little bit of the best of everything, from everywhere.

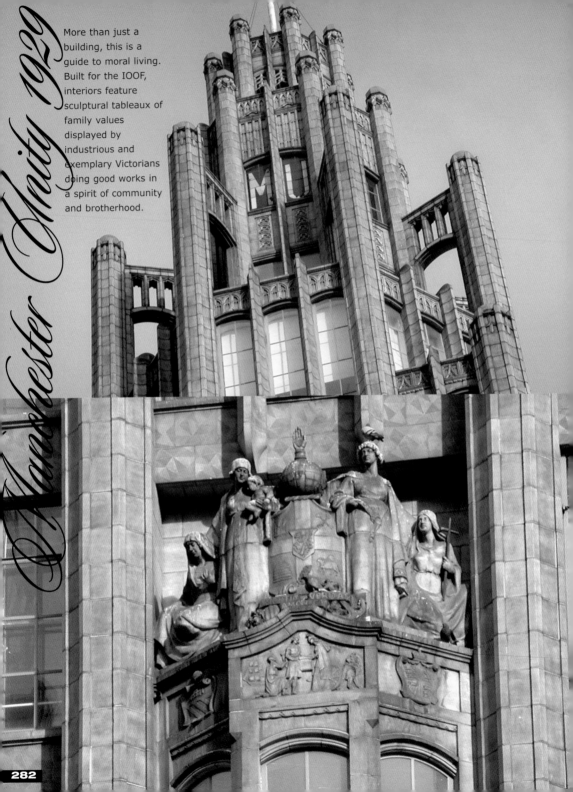

More than just a building, this is a guide to moral living. Built for the IOOF, interiors feature sculptural tableaux of family values displayed by industrious and exemplary Victorians doing good works in a spirit of community and brotherhood.

Metropolitan Fire Station 1893

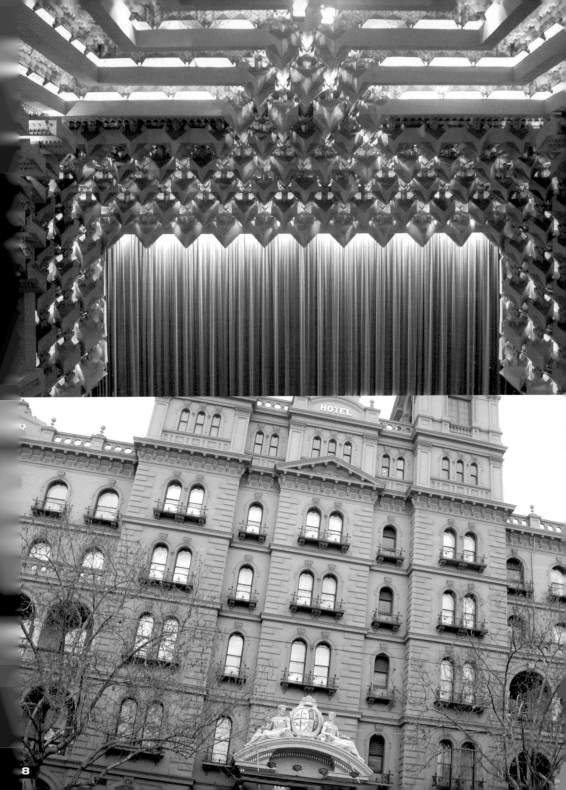

Architecture

The

Built in 1883, this Gothic revival masterpiece is now owned by the ANZ Bank. Originally the English Scottish & Australian Bank — ES&A — it is a testament to the impact of the gold boom. Architect William Wardell and banker Sir George Verdon gave it everything they had, creating their most spectacular, ornate, and blatant tribute to the overnight inundation of wealth that was the instant making of Melbourne. The skylight (previous pages) was added in the 1920s. The Stock Exchange building next door, designed by architect William Pitt, was incorporated into the bank in 1950.

The Stock Exchange

Theatres

Melbourne's picture palaces and theatres of the 1920s, 30s and 40s are some of the world's finest examples of popular, ornate design. Burley Griffin's Capitol Cinema, The Forum, the Regent, the Plaza, the Princess...Melbourne boasts a whole collection of rare architectural gems. The Regent/Plaza is now fully restored, while others still patiently await their turn for a makeover.

The story of the Regent Theatre reads like a fairy tale. It started life as a glittering FAIRY PRINCESS. Born into the Great Depression in 1929, it closed, reopened and struggled for many years. It was eventually sold to the Melbourne City Council in 1969 who, intending to demolish it for a modern high-rise, gutted the building and sold off the exquisite fittings from its ornate interiors. As a neglected CINDERELLA it suffered at the mercy of others, until saved from demolition by controversial labour unionist Norm Gallagher. BEAUTY AND THE BEAST take over from here, with Gallagher as the theatre's champion. It was he who first saw the heritage value of this and other major architectural treasures. He instituted 'green bans' in the early 1970s preventing his Builders Labourers Federation members from demolishing this marvellous theatre, along with the City Baths, the Queen Victoria Market, and historic terrace housing rows in Carlton. Gallagher was a formidable opponent, frustrating governments and developers alike until eventually succeeding in saving the theatre. But then the Regent languished in disuse, empty and forgotten for 24 years, becoming THE SLEEPING BEAUTY of Collins Street. In 1996, after a government injection of some $12 million, the Regent Theatre reopened its doors fully refurbished by new owner Marriner Theatres. As CINDERELLA restored to her full glory, the Regent Theatre now sparkles brighter than ever.

Regent Theatre 1929

ELBOURNE'S 'PALACE OF DREAMS', THE REGENT THEATRE, WAS BUILT IN 1929
R FLAMBOYANT THEATRICAL ENTREPRENEUR AND ACTOR F.W. THRING. IT IS
ADY, ORNATE, SUMPTUOUS, ROCOCO EXTRAVAGANCE AT ITS FINEST.

303

The Forum Theatre 1928

'By a clever illusion, an imitation Mediterranean sky, with twinkling stars and a gibbous moon, takes the place of an ordinary canopied roof, so that patrons can if they like, imagine themselves seated out-of-doors.'
The Argus *newspaper,*
January 1929

FLINDERS STREET STATION

Conforming to the agreed gauge width decided by NSW, Victoria built its rail lines to the broad gauge of 5 feet 3 inches. But NSW went on to make the change to a 4 feet 6 inches width, making a uniform national system impossible.

FL

and
E LINES

FRANKSTON
LINE

PLATFORM

NEXT TRAIN FOR

FLINDERS STREET STATION

On a site originally occupied by a fish market, Melbourne's first rail station at Flinders Street was built in 1854. A group of weatherboard sheds known as Melbourne Terminus, it served the nation's first rail line from Sandridge (Port Melbourne) to the city and was run by the Melbourne & Hobson's Bay Railway Co. (M&HBRCo). Later, the Melbourne Terminus and M&HBRCo handled the suburban south-eastern lines, while the government-owned Victorian Railways (VR) and Spencer Street Station took care of the northern and country lines.

In 1878, VR purchased the privately owned M&HBRCo, and in 1905, the present Flinders Street building was constructed. The winner of an architectural competition, the Edwardian baroque design is the work of two railway employees, Fawcett and Ashworth. A stunning example of its architectural type, it contained in its interior a surprising variety of facilities, and has over the century served the people of Melbourne as landmark, rail station, meeting place and much more.

The public facilities included a Children's Nursery opened in 1933, where for sixpence an hour or two shillings a day women could leave their children while they shopped in the city. With '...cots for babies... a rockinghorse, toys, unsplinterable glass...' and a staff of experienced nurses, this was great value. The third floor housed extensive facilities available to Victorian Railways Institute members in this extraordinary workplace. These included a large concert hall, a billiard room, a gymnasium with sauna, games room, reference and lending library, reading and smoking rooms and two classrooms. Fifteen meeting rooms were made available for hire to outside groups, including '...cat-lovers, rose devotees, former residents of country towns, dog drivers, fuel merchants, piscatorial enthusiasts, talented debaters, ex-servicemen, [and] poetry lovers...' and in later years the Chihuahua Club, Collingwood Cheer Squad, and the Women's Action Committee.

The ballroom held regular dances and social evenings right up until the 1970s when rock'n'roll lured people elsewhere. From then on it had regular bookings by the Youth Hostel Association, Widows and Widowers groups, and 'Saturday Dances for lonely people', held by Father Glover, but was available for hire on any Tuesday night for just $30.

After nearly 150 years of public ownership, the Kennett government privatised Melbourne's rail system in August 1999 after funding a $28 million redevelopment of the main entry and concourse. Two companies now known as Connex (a French company, owned along with Universal Studios, by Vivendi Universal) and M Trains (owned by Britain's National Express) share the running of Melbourne's trains and stations, with the landmark Flinders Street Station controlled by Connex, whose franchise for operation of the rolling stock and station buildings has a term of 15 years.

And so, at the beginning of the 21st century, Flinders Street Station, its history and its future, are in foreign care until 2014. Once so vitally possessed by Melburnians, this landmark represents the contrast between a past golden age of endless workplace facilities, and the harsh realities of privatisation.

Flinders Street's No. 1 platform is the longest rail platform in Australia, at over 700 m.

sculpture

THE MAGIC PUDDING BY LOUIS LAUMEN, IAN POTTER FOUNDATION CHILDREN'S GARDEN

sculpture

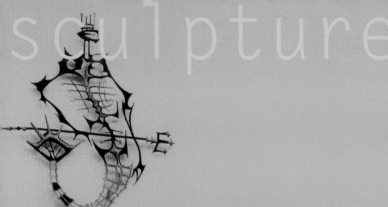

Sculpture is a measure of the civility of a place. Expensive, unconcerned with the fundamental needs of a city, it can be hard to justify, labelled vainglorious and unnecessary. But unlike painted works of art, sculpture stands in our everyday places. It belongs to us all, to ponder, admire or reject. Its presence means there is effort being made to reflect on higher themes: like history and humanity, place and identity. And sculpture is also a measure of the value a city places on beauty. For who or whatever the subject of the work may be, the artist is also there. In Melbourne's streets grand and historic commissions combine with corporate adornments to give the city plenty of artistic food for thought. Sublime talents are called to capture sublime events. They also manufacture icons to beautify the mundane. A level above architecture in its gifts to the soul, sculpture is the ultimate celebration of place, just for the art of it.

OR TRUMPER BY LOUIS LAUMEN

THE SWIMMER BY JEFFREY WILKINSON

sculpture

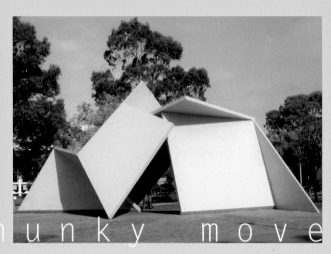

chunky moves

Almost instantly dubbed 'the Yellow Peril', Ron Robertson-Swann's 'Vault' of 1978 is a surprisingly moving work. Dogged by controversy, 'Vault' has become as important a part of Melbourne's urban mythology as it has of its landscape. Originally sited in the centre of Melbourne's City Square, it immediately attracted debate and disdain. Like much abstract formalist art, it seemed either inscrutible or just too simple to laymen, who felt they could do as well. Due to either its unpopularity or its ability to shelter homeless people, it was moved, and moved again, each time further from the critical glare of passers-by. Each move has meant the unhinging and reassembly of seven enormous welded steel plates. Rejected from location after location, this controversial work was finally unofficially civically 'disowned', when under the cover of darkness in 1981 'Vault' was relocated to the then unkempt and unfrequented Batman Park on the Yarra. Twenty years later, the increasingly well-groomed and well-frequented Batman Park (above) had gained an expensive new neighbour in the Crown Casino and Entertainment Complex, putting 'Vault' once again, accidentally, at the centre of things. But, never still for long, 'Vault' was moved again from Melbourne's popular redeveloped riverside to a new home at the all-new Centre for Contemporary Arts at South Melbourne in 2002. While the original sculpture cost $70,000 to create, this latest move cost $90,000 to execute. It seems this most recent relocation is evidence at last that Melbourne is finally ready for 'Vault' and has embraced it as an elite and essential feature of Melbourne's creative landscape.

VAULT

the yellow peril

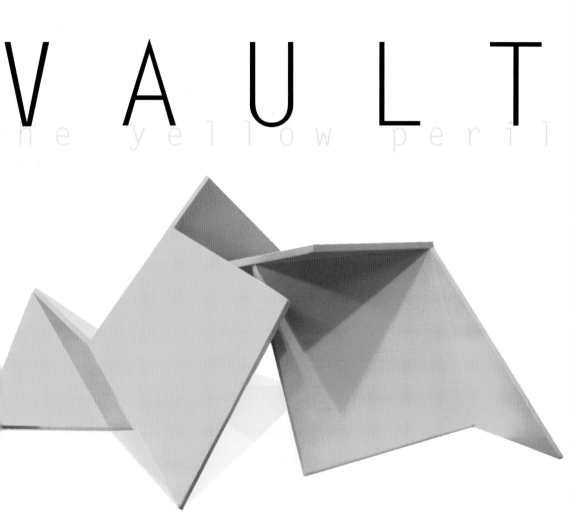

THE ORIGINAL WORKING MODEL FOR 'VAULT', NOW HELD AT THE McCLELLAND GALLERY, LANGWARRIN

WIPERS AND THE DRIVER BY C. SARGEANT JA[C]

SALI CLEVE DRINKING FOUNTAIN BY J. MARRIOT

sculpture

is easy. Beginning with around 800 kilos of clay, sculptor Louis Laumen simply removes everything that doesn't look like a football game. Then he and a team of six craftsmen at the 'Fonderie' in Melbourne's Richmond, paint the modelled clay figures with a coating of rubber to make a mould. This is strengthened with a fibreglass backing to keep it rigid. The mould is then carefully cut away in sections, and the white clay sculpture inside is crushed up for reuse. The inside of the mould is then painted with an $\frac{1}{8}$ inch coating of wax (this will be replaced with the final layer of bronze) and the mould is reassembled with the waxed layer inside. The core is then filled with a slurry of plaster and brick dust, which sets hard. The rubber mould is peeled away, leaving the waxed layer on the outside of the solid core, and any dents and dags on the wax are retouched and repaired. Next, the waxed exterior is covered in a 'clay' which will become a ceramic shell after firing in the kiln. It is fired until the clay is baked hard and the layer of wax is melted away. This leaves a paper-thin empty layer where the wax was sandwiched between the ceramic 'clay' and the core. Into this empty layer is poured molten bronze, which fills every nook and cranny, conforming to the surface textures of the inside of the ceramic shell. This is all allowed to cool. If the pour is successful,

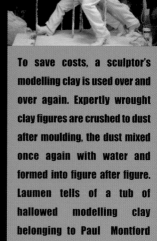

To save costs, a sculptor's modelling clay is used over and over again. Expertly wrought clay figures are crushed to dust after moulding, the dust mixed once again with water and formed into figure after figure. Laumen tells of a tub of hallowed modelling clay belonging to Paul Montford (sculptor of the Shrine, 1930s) that eventually found its way to the studio of Stanley Hammond whose Collins Street figure of John Pascoe Fawkner may literally be made of the same stuff as the ANZACs.

then begins the tedious process of chipping away the outer ceramic to reveal the bronze, and the hollowing out of the brickdust clay core inside. Then comes filing, buffing, polishing and even tinting of the bronze surface to leave nothing that is not worthy of the word 'masterpiece'. The entire process took Laumen six months including research, sketches, miniatures (maquettes), modelling, casting and finishing. Easy.

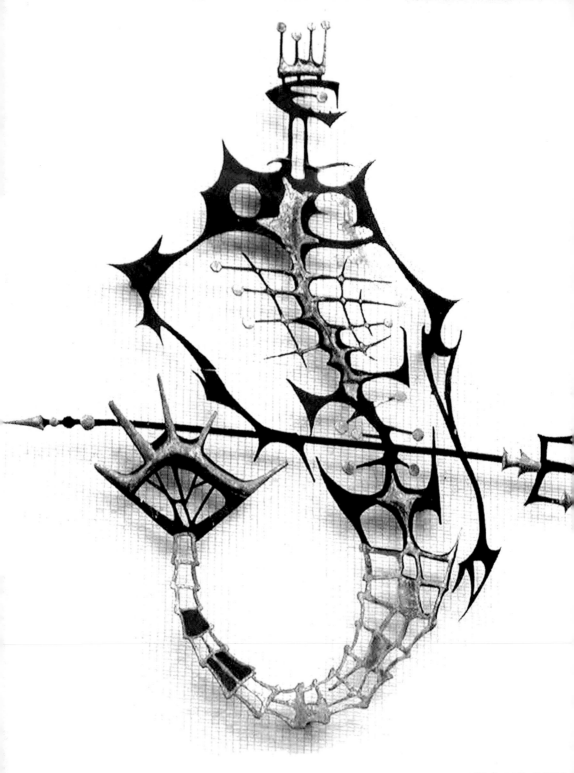

PORT PHILLIP ARCADE

In the decade from 1980 to 1990, seven CBD sculptures were commissioned.
From 1990 to 1998, the number of sculptures commissioned for Melbourne's CBD had jumped to 50.

Diana and her hounds
W. Leslie Bowles 1940
Fitzroy Gardens

sculpture

As yet there's no statue of Dame Nellie **MELBA** in the main street of Melbourne. Nor one of **ETHEL (HENRY HANDEL) RICHARDSON,** author of *The Fortunes of Richard Mahoney*. In a city obsessed with sport there is no statue of gold medal winning 1956 Melbourne Olympic swimmer **FAITH LEECH**, swimmers **JUDY JOY DAVIES** and **MARJORIE McQUADE**, or diver **BARBARA McCAULEY**. No statue of the composer of the first Australian opera **MARGARET SUTHERLAND**, or writer and editor **MAIE CASEY**. Or Melbourne's first female impressionist painter **JANE SUTHERLAND**. Or Heide's **JOY HESTER**. No **VIDA GOLDSTEIN** or **BELLA GUERIN**, suffragettes and social reformers. No **JEANNIE GUNN**, Melbourne author of *We of the Never-Never*. Not even pioneer aristocrat and artist **GEORGIANA MACRAE.** If racehorse breeder Bart Cummings' statue is erected during his own lifetime, then why not **GERMAINE GREER**'s in hers? A recent sculptural tribute to Port Melbourne Senator **OLIVE ZAKHAROV** is a non-figurative abstract made of three concrete blocks, so there's no chance of knowing it celebrates a real woman who once had form and shape, and who once shaped Melbourne.

With all this talent in Melbourne's history, it shouldn't be so hard to find a good woman, sculpturally speaking. And yet at the dawn of the 21st century, there is only one statue of a Melbourne woman in Melbourne city. The modest bronze torso of **MARY GILBERT**, only female settler among the first white party of 1835, is so unprepossessing it's easy to miss. Sculpted by Ailsa O'Connor in 1974, it occasionally stands among the floral exhibits inside the Fitzroy Gardens Conservatory as part of a rotation of displays. In between displays, Gilbert's statue is stored unceremoniously in a junk-filled gardener's shed, where she is even easier to miss. There is nothing grand or pompous in this portrayal of Mary Gilbert. Her right hand is bandaged in her 19th-century skirts while her left hand has been severely damaged by a more contemporary mishap in handling.

As the only woman in a difficult and often brutal fledgling Melbourne in 1835, Gilbert's story fires the imagination. But perhaps even more interesting is that after 170 years, Mary Gilbert is still alone in this city, as the only Melbourne woman to have achieved statue status. There are bronzed Aussie blokes on every corner, and Melbourne proudly displays France's Joan of Arc, Italy's Saint Catherine, Britain's Nurse Edith Cavell and Diana from the mythical Roman pantheon. But, nymphs and nudes notwithstanding, there is just this one part-time, diminutive half-figure to mark the women of Melbourne's own history. When the pendulum finally swings, however, at least we can be sure there are plenty of great women to choose from.

MELBOURNE SCULPTOR MARGARET BASKERVILLE
WAS THE FIRST WOMAN COMMISSIONED TO
CREATE PUBLIC SCULPTURE IN VICTORIA AND WAS
WIDELY COMMISSIONED IN AUSTRALIA FROM 1910
UNTIL HER DEATH IN 1930. HER WORKS INCLUDE
THIS BUST OF BRITISH NURSE EDITH CAVELL, 1926,
AND A BRONZE FIGURE OF THOMAS BENT, 1913.

Jeanne d'Arc

'Jeanne d'Arc' is a bronze replica of a statue by the French sculptor Emmanuel Fremiet (1824–1910). The original was erected in the Place des Pyramides, Paris, in 1899. This replica was purchased with money from the Felton Bequest and was erected at the State Library in 1907. There are other replicas in both France and in the United States.

SCULPTURE FINDER

VICTOR TRUMPER
by LOUIS LAUMEN 1999
@ MCG – Private commission
currently on loan to the MCG

MAN WITH THE DONKEY
by WALLACE ANDERSON
1936
@ Shrine of Remembrance

BIRTH OF THE GAME
by LOUIS LAUMEN 2001
@ MCG

SHRINE OF
REMEMBRANCE
by Paul MONTFORD
1928–1934
@ Shrine of Remembrance

THE MAGIC PUDDING
by LOUIS LAUMEN 2000
@ Ian Potter Foundation
Children's Garden

PETER PAN
by PAUL MONTFORD 1925
@ Melbourne Zoo

WIDOW AND CHILDREN
by LOUIS LAUMEN 1998
@ Shrine of Remembrance

MACPHERSON ROBERTSON
FOUNTAIN
by PAUL MONTFORD/PHILIP
HUDSON 1934
@ Shrine Gardens

ST CATHERINE OF SIENA
by LOUIS LAUMEN 2000
@ St Patrick's Cathedral

ADAM LINDSAY GORDON
by PAUL MONTFORD 1931
@ Gordon Reserve

ST FRANCIS OF ASSISI
by LOUIS LAUMEN 2000
@ St Patrick's Cathedral

WATER NYMPH
by PAUL MONTFORD 1925
@ Queen Victoria Gardens

SCULPTURE FINDER

JOHN BATMAN
by STANLEY HAMMOND
1978
@ Collins Street

BARON FERDINAND VON
MUELLER
by MARC CLARK 1985
@ Royal Botanic Gardens

EIGHT-HOUR DAY
by PERCIVAL BALL 1903
@ Queens Park

THE SALI CLEVE DRINKING
FOUNTAIN
by J. MARRIOT 1911
@ St Kilda Foreshore

ST GEORGE & THE DRAGON
by SIR EDGAR BOEHM 1888
@ State Library of Victoria

QUEEN VICTORIA
by JAMES WHITE 1907
@ Queen Victoria Gardens

JEANNE D'ARC
by EMMANUEL FREMIET
1907
@ State Library of Victoria

BURKE AND WILLS
by CHARLES SUMMERS 1865
@ Cnr Collins/Swanston Sts

THE CHILDREN'S TREE
by TOM BASS 1953
@ Cnr Collins/Elizabeth Sts

WIPERS (YPRES)
by C. SARGEANT JAGGER 1937
@ Shrine of Remembrance

GENIE
by TOM BASS 1973
@ Queen Victoria Gardens

THE DRIVER
by C. SARGEANT JAGGER
1937
@ Shrine of Remembrance

sculpture

THE PATHFINDER
by JOHN ROBINSON 1974
@ Queen Victoria Gardens

EXHIBITION FOUNTAIN
by HOCHGURTEL 1880
@ Exhibition Buildings

NURSE CAVELL
by MARGARET BASKERVILLE
1926
@ Kings Domain

FRENCH FOUNTAIN
SCULPTOR UNKNOWN
@ Exhibition Buildings

DERVISH
by CLEMENT MEADMORE
@ Southbank

KING GEORGE V MEMORIAL
1937–1952
by W. LESLIE BOWLES
@ Kings Domain

OPHELIA
by DEBORAH HALPERN
1992
@ Southbank

KING GEORGE V MEMORIAL
'BRITANNIA'
by W. LESLIE BOWLES
1937–1952
@ Kings Domain

ANGEL
by DEBORAH HALPERN
1987–89
@ National Gallery of Victoria

DIANA AND THE HOUNDS
by W. LESLIE BOWLES 1940
@ Fitzroy Gardens

WESTGARTH DRINKING
FOUNTAIN
SCULPTOR UNKNOWN
1888
@ Exhibition Buildings

EDWARD VII
SCULPTOR UNKNOWN
1920
@ Queen Victoria Gardens

SCULPTURE FINDER

CAPT MATTHEW FLINDERS
by CHARLES WEBB GILBERT
1925
@ St Pauls Cathedral

APOLLO
c. 1780, erected 1928
@ Queen Victoria Gardens

BURKE AND WILLS
by CHARLES SUMMERS 1865
@ Cnr Collins/Swanston Sts

FAMEX HERCULES
c. 1780, erected 1928
@ Queen Victoria Gardens

EARL OF HOPETOUN &
MARQUIS OF LINLITHGOW
by WILLIAM BIRNIE RHIND
1911
@ Kings Domain

ARCHBISHOP MANNIX
by NIGEL BOONHAM 1999
@ St Patricks Cathedral

JOHN PASCOE FAWKNER
by MICHAEL MEZAROS
1979
@ Collins Street

DANIEL O'CONNELL
by THOMAS BROCK
of London 1888
@ St Patricks Cathedral

THE GUILFOYLE MEMORIAL
SCULPTURE
by MICHAEL MEZAROS
1998
@ Royal Botanic Gardens

PHARLAP
by PETER CORLETT 1988
@ Flemington Race Course

SIDNEY MYER
by MICHAEL MEZAROS
2001
@ Myer Music Bowl

WEARY DUNLOP
by PETER CORLETT 1995
@ Kings Domain

sculpture

ATLAS
SCULPTOR UNKNOWN
@ Guardian Royal Exchange
Assurance (Formerly Atlas
Assurance) Building
Collins Street

VAULT
by RON ROBERTSON-SWANN
1978
@ Australian Centre for
Contemporary Art,
South Melbourne

MONUMENT TO THE 5TH
CONTINGENT
by architect George de Lucy
and sculptor Joseph Hamilton
1903
@ St Kilda Road

TRIBUTE TO OLIVE ZAKHAROV
by CHIMERA COLLECTIONS
2002
@ Olive's Corner, Liardet
Street, Port Melbourne

MARY GILBERT
by AILSA O'CONNOR 1974
@ Fitzroy Gardens
Conservatory

EAGLE
by BRUCE ARMSTRONG
2002
@ Wurundjeri Way

WEATHER VANES
by DANIEL JENKINS 1993
@ Cnr Bourke/Swanston Sts
1 of 4: bird, horse, fish, pig

COW UP A TREE
by JOHN KELLY 1991
@ Harbour Esplanade,
Docklands

PORT PHILLIP ARCADE MOTIF
SCULPTOR UNKNOWN
1961
@ 234 Flinders Street

WEATHER VANE
SCULPTOR UNKNOWN
1919
@ Missions to Seamen
Flinders Street

THE HOUSE IN THE SKY
by urban designers
BREARLEY MIDDLETON 2001
@ Western Ring Road,
Laverton North

GARDEN OF UNITY
by AKIO MAKIGAWA 2001
@ Royal Exhibition Gardens

SCULPTURE FINDER

THE SWIMMER
by JEFFREY WILKINSON
Original maquette c. 1950
Bronze by BRUCE CLAYTON
1999
@ Hampton Foreshore

SEAL SCULPTURE
by PETER CORLETT and
LOUISE SKACEJ 1987
@ Melbourne Zoo

CAPT JAMES COOK
by MARC CLARK
1974
@ Fitzroy Gardens

FEDERATION BELLS
2001
by ANTON HASELL
@ Birrarung Marr Park

ARCHITECTURAL FRAGMENT
by PETRUS SPRONK 1993
@ State Library Victoria

THE PUBLIC PURSE
by SIMON PERRY 1994
@ Bourke Street Mall

THE BOER WAR MONUMENT
by architects IRWIN &
STEPHENSON 1924
@ St Kilda Road

MELBOURNE

DETAILS

PICTURE CREDITS & ACKNOWLEDGMENTS

p.8 Melbourne Map, La Trobe Picture Collection, State Library of Victoria (Reproduced in *Picture Book of Australiasia When* by Cedric Flower, Golden Press, 1978) **p.10** Lt. Gov. David Collins, La Trobe Collection, State Library of Victoria (Reproduced in *The Chronicles of Early Melbourne, 1835 to 1852: Historical Anecdotal and Personal by 'Garryowen'* by Edmund Finn (1819-1898), Centennial ed. Melbourne, Heritage Publications, 1976) **p.12** John Pascoe Fawkner by William Strutt, La Trobe Collection, State Library of Victoria **p.13** *Top:* John Batman, La Trobe Collection, State Library of Victoria (Reproduced in *The Chronicles of Early Melbourne, 1835 to 1852: Historical Anecdotal and Personal by 'Garryowen'* by Edmund Finn (1819-1898), Centennial ed. Melbourne, Heritage Publications, 1976); *Centre:* John Batman and the Aborigines, La Trobe Collection, State Library of Victoria (Reproduced in *Melbourne An Illustrated History* by Brian Carroll, Lansdowne Press, Melbourne, 1972) **p.14** William Lamb, Lord Melbourne, La Trobe Collection, State Library of Victoria (Reproduced in *The Chronicles of Early Melbourne, 1835 to 1852: Historical Anecdotal and Personal by 'Garryowen'* by Edmund Finn (1819-1898), Centennial ed. Melbourne, Heritage Publications, 1976) **p.16** Melbourne Land Allotments, La Trobe Collection, State Library of Victoria (Reproduced in *The Colonial Experience* by Barbara Vance Wilson, Oxford University Press, Melbourne,1990) **p.20** Buckley's Cave by Jan Senbergs, 1996, courtesy of the artist and Sharon Grey **p.22** Portrait of Buckley by unknown artist, La Trobe Collection, State Library of Victoria **p.24** William Buckley by W. Macleod, La Trobe Collection, State Library of Victoria (Reproduced in *Melbourne An Illustrated History* by Brian Carroll, Lansdowne Press, Melbourne, 1972) **p.26** Buckley's Cave (detail) by Jan Senbergs, 1996, courtesy of the artist and Sharon Grey **p.31** Blackfellow Painted for a Corroboree, *Sun Pictures of Victoria 1858* by Antoine Fauchery, La Trobe Picture Collection, State Library of Victoria (Reproduced in *Sun Pictures of Victoria, the Fauchery–Daintree Collection 1858* by Dianne Reilly and Jennifer Carew, Curry, O'Neill, Ross, Melbourne, 1983) **p.35** Batman's Treaty Document, La Trobe Australian Manuscripts Collection, State Library of Victoria **p.37** Group of Blackfellows (detail), *Sun Pictures of Victoria 1858* by Antoine Fauchery, La Trobe Picture Collection, State Library of Victoria (Reproduced in *Sun Pictures of Victoria, the Fauchery–Daintree Collection 1858* by Dianne Reilly and Jennifer Carew, Curry, O'Neill, Ross, Melbourne, 1983) **p.40** *Top:* Aborigines Chasing Chinese: Hunting Scene by Tommy McCrae, Museum of Victoria (Reproduced in *Aboriginal Artists of the Nineteenth Century* by Andrew Sayers, Oxford University Press, Melbourne, 1994); *Bottom:* Lachlan War Dance by Tommy McCrae, La Trobe Collection, State Library of Victoria (Reproduced in *Aboriginal Artists of the Nineteenth Century* by Andrew Sayers, Oxford University Press, Melbourne, 1994) **p.41** Buckley Ran Away from the Ship by Tommy McCrae, c. 1870, pen and ink on paper, courtesy Koorie Heritage Trust Inc Collection. **p.42** Self Portrait (detail) by Antoine Fauchery, *Sun Pictures of Victoria 1858*, La Trobe Picture Collection, State Library of Victoria (Reproduced in *Sun Pictures of Victoria, the Fauchery–Daintree Collection 1858* by Dianne Reilly and Jennifer Carew, Curry, O'Neill, Ross, Melbourne, 1983) **p.43** Portrait of Mirka Mora by Geoffrey Smith, courtesy Virginia Edwards **p.46** Melbourne's Wharf by Francois Cogne, La Trobe Picture Collection, State Library of Victoria **p.47** Portrait of Antoine Fauchery by unknown artist, La Trobe Collection, State Libary of Victoria. (Reproduced in *Sun Pictures of Victoria, the Fauchery–Daintree Collection 1858* by Dianne Reilly and Jennifer Carew, Curry, O'Neill, Ross, Melbourne, 1983) **p.49** Self Portrait by Antoine Fauchery, *Sun Pictures of Victoria 1858*, La Trobe Picture Collection, State Library of Victoria (Reproduced in *Sun Pictures of Victoria, the Fauchery–Daintree Collection 1858* by Dianne Reilly and Jennifer Carew, Curry, O'Neill, Ross, Melbourne, 1983) **p.54** Parliament House Victoria, courtesy Parliament House Library Committee **p.64–65** *Top:* A Design for Arms for the Colony of Victoria by William Strutt, courtesy Parliament House Library Committee (Reproduced in *Victoria the Golden, Scenes Sketches and Jottings from Nature 1850-1862* by William Strutt) **p.64** *Bottom:* Study for Coat of Arms by William Strutt, courtesy Parliament House Library Committee **p.65** *Centre:* Arms for the City of Melbourne by William Strutt, courtesy Parliament House Library Committee; *Bottom:* Victorian Coat of Arms, Armorial Ensign, with permission of the Victorian State Government **p.72** Melba Commemorative Issue stamp, 1961, La Trobe Collection, State Library of Victoria (Reproduced in *Melbourne an Illustrated History* by Brian Carroll, Lansdowne Press, Melbourne, 1972) **p.73** Australia Madame Melba (detail) by Rupert Bunny (1864–1947), c. 1902, oil on canvas, 245.5 cm x 153.0 cm (Purchased through The Art Foundation of VIctoria with the assistance of Dinah and Henry Krongold, CBE, Founder Benefactors, 1980, National Gallery of Australia) **p.74** Portrait of Sidney Myer by John Longstaff,

PICTURE CREDITS & ACKNOWLEDGMENTS

reproduced with permission, courtesy Myer Family Trust **p.77** Myer Bendigo, reproduced with permission, courtesy Myer Family Trust. La Trobe Collection, State Library of Victoria (Reproduced in *The Gay Provider, The Myer Story* by Alan Marshall, Cheshire, Melbourne, 1961) **p.77** Wright & Neil drapery, reproduced with permission, courtesy Myer Family Trust. La Trobe Collection, State Library of Victoria. (Reproduced in *The Gay Provider, The Myer Story* by Alan Marshall, Cheshire, Melbourne, 1961) **p.81** Melbourne Land Allotments, La Trobe Collection, State Library of Victoria (Reproduced in *The Colonial Experience* by Barbara Vance Wilson, Oxford University Press, Melbourne, 1990) **p.100–101** The Botanic Gardens by Francois Cogne, c. 1863, La Trobe Picture Collection, State Library of Victoria (Reproduced in *Melbourne Album, Melbourne 1863* by Charles Troedel, and in *The Melbourne Scene 1803-1956* by James Grant & Geoffrey Serle, first published by Melbourne University Press, Melbourne, 1957, reprinted by Hale & Ironmonger, 1978) **p.126** *Bottom left:* (Liardet's Pier) First Landing Place at Sandridge 1840, La Trobe Collection, State Library of Victoria (Reproduced in *Victoria Today, a Review 1851–1901* and in *A History of Port Melbourne*, by Nancy U'ren and Noel Turnbull, Oxford University Press, Melbourne, 1983) *Top right:* Approach to Melbourne 1844, La Trobe Collection, State Library of Victoria (Reproduced in *Port of Melbourne, 1835–1976* by Olaf Ruhen, Cassell, Stanmore, New South Wales, 1976) **p.132–133** Study for the Yarra River, 1991, by Wendy Foard, reproduced with the artist's permission and courtesy Libby Ross **p.143** *Bottom left:* Native Dignity by S. T. Gill, La Trobe Picture Collection, State Library of Victoria (Reproduced in *White on Black, the Australian Aborigine Portrayed in Art* by Geoffrey Dutton, Macmillan, South. Melbourne, 1974) *Top right:* The Savage Club Bookplate by David Low, courtesy The Melbourne Savage Club. La Trobe Collection, State Library of Victoria (Reproduced in *Melbourne Savages a History of the First 50 Years* by David Dow, Melbourne Savage Club, Melbourne, 1947) **p.157** *Top left:* Upper Yarra water catchment, courtesy Melbourne Water **p.169** Portrait of Phillip Adams, courtesy Mr Adams and his management **p.171** *Top:* Melbourne Map, La Trobe Collection, State Library of Victoria (Reproduced in *Picture Book of Australiasia When* by Cedric Flower, Golden Press, 1978); *Bottom:* Sydney Map, La Trobe Collection, State Library of Victoria. (Reproduced in *Picture Book of Australiasia When* by Cedric Flower, Golden Press, 1978) **p.172** Portrait of Kerry

Armstrong, courtesy Ms Armstrong and her management **p.174** *Centre:* Christmas at Heide, copyright Estate of Albert Tucker, courtesy Lauraine Diggins Fine Art and Heide Museum of Modern Art; *Right:* In the Library, copyright Estate of Albert Tucker, courtesy Lauraine Diggins Fine Art and Heide Museum of Modern Art **p.176** Tokens from *Coles Funny Picture Book No. 3*, Cole Publications, Melbourne, 1951 **p.177** *Top left:* Arcade exterior from *Coles Funny Picture Book No.3*, Cole Publications, Melbourne, 1951, used with permission, courtesy Cole Publications; *Top right:* Cover design of one of Cole's earlier pamphlets 'Information for the People on the Religions of the World' (Reproduced in *Cole of the Book Arcade, a biography of E.W.Cole* by Cole Turnley, Cole Publications, Melbourne, 1974). Used with permission, courtesy Cole Publications; *Bottom left:* Testimonials to the Astonishing Curing Power of Cole's Fun Doctor (Reproduced in *Coles Funny Picture Book No.1*, Cole Publications, first published Melbourne, 1879, reproduced in 74th ed., Melbourne, 1983). Used with permission, courtesy Cole Publications; *Bottom right:* Interior of Coles Book Arcade as depicted in the Melbourne Directory of 1888 (Reproduced in *Cole of the Book Arcade, a biography of E.W.Cole* by Cole Turnley, Cole Publications, Melbourne, 1974). Used with permission, courtesy Cole Publications **p.178–179** The True History of the Great Sea Serpent from *Coles Funny Picture Book No.1*, Cole Publications, first published Melbourne, 1879, reproduced in 74th ed., Melbourne, 1983. Used with permission, courtesy Cole Publications **p.181** Tom Wills and the Aboriginal Australian Side (detail), courtesy Melbourne Cricket Club Museum **p.183** Tom Wills and the Aboriginal Australian Side, courtesy Melbourne Cricket Club Museum **p.191** Portrait of Vince Colosimo courtesy Mr Colosimo and his management **p.194–195** The *Argus* masthead, Newspapers Collection, State Library of Victoria **p.194** Big Ned, used with permission, courtesy Glenrowan Post Office **p.200–201** Ute images, courtesy Ford Australia **p.202** Archival jars, courtesy Kraft Foods, Melbourne **p.208–209** The Lawn, Flemington (detail) by Carl Kahler, 1888, La Trobe Collection, State Library of Victoria (Reproduced in *The Glorious Years* by Graeme Inson and Russell Ward, Jacaranda, Queensland, 1971) **p.210** *Top row left:* Michelle Bartoli wearing David Medwin design, used with permission; *3rd row left and right:* Chintha Panditaratne, courtesy Maya Kalan Millinery; *Bottom row centre,* Rochelle Foster wearing J'Aton, courtesy Chadwick Management **p.211** Michelle Bartoli wearing David Medwin design, used with

PICTURE CREDITS & ACKNOWLEDGMENTS

permission p.**212, 213, 216, 217** Crown TV campaign, images courtesy Crown and the creators. Campaign designed and written by Maree Coote for John Singleton Advertising, Melbourne 1997; directed by Graeme Burfoot for Film Graphics; produced by Jude Lengel and Liz Conway; CGI (Computer Generated Imagery) by Animal Logic; Music by Chong Lim; starring Tom Beaumont as the Jester, with Kate, Cindy, Cecily, Paula, Rikke, Max, Steven, Kent, Nick and Josedy from Chadwick Management, with Rebecca from Giant, James from Viviens and introducing Melbourne's entire community of street performers. Costume design by Graeme Burfoot, Maree Coote and Jenny Sant with stylists Wendy Bannister, Peter Jago and Deborah McLean. Hair and make-up by Ruth Sebire and Gay Gallagher; choreography by Helen Herbertson; props and set design by Martin O'Neill; second unit director Kent Allen p.**214** Melbourne Map, La Trobe Collection, State Library of Victoria (Reproduced in *Picture Book of Australiasia When* by Cedric Flower, Golden Press, 1978) p.**226** *Left*: Princess Panda, image used with permission; *Bottom*: Scenes from Graham Kennedy's IMT, courtesy Channel 9 p.**231, 232, 234** Graham Kennedy from Graham Kennedy's IMT, Cinemedia Film Archive, used with permission courtesy Nine Network p.**233** Graham Kennedy and Bert Newton, 1964, photo by Barrie Bell, courtesy Nine Network. Used with permission, courtesy Mr Kennedy and Mr Newton p.**235** *Top row centre*: courtesy Mr Philip Brady and Nine Network; *2nd row left*: Graham Kennedy's IMT, Cinemedia Film Archive, used with permission; *2nd row right*: Molly Meldrum, with permission, courtesy ABCTV and Mr Meldrum; *3rd row centre*: Photo by Peter English, 1961, courtesy Nine Network; *Bottom row left*: Photo by Chris Whitehorn,1960, courtesy Nine Network; *Bottom row right*: courtesy Mr Philip Brady and Nine

Network p.**250** Portrait of Effie aka Mary Coustas courtesy Seven Network and Nannette Fox p.**253** Portrait of Helena Rubinstein by William Dobell (1899-1970) Australia, 1957, oil on composition board, 95.4 cm x 95.6 cm, Felton Bequest, 1964, National Gallery of Victoria, Melbourne p.**259** Photo of Jenny Bannister Parade by Brad Hicks 2002 , courtesy Melbourne Fashion Festival p.**263** *2nd row centre*: 'Gladiator' by Jenny Bannister, photo courtesy Ms Bannister p.**264** *Far left*: The Lawn, Flemington (detail), by Carl Kahler, 1888, La Trobe Collection, State Library of Victoria (Reproduced in *The Glorious Years* by Graeme Inson and Russell Ward, Jacaranda, Queensland, 1971 p.**265** *Left and centre*: Artwork by Robert Pearce; *Far right*: Artwork by Studio Anybody, courtesy Melbourne Fashion Festival p.**267** Uncombined portrait of Robert Buckingham, courtesy Melbourne Fashion Festival p.**268–269** Photos by Eric Blaich, 1997, used with permission p.**270** Portrait of Lillian Wightman by unknown photographer, courtesy Le Louvre archives p.**271** *Top row right*: Dame Edna Everage wearing Le Louvre, courtesy Mr Barry Humphries and Peter Isaacson Publications Pty Ltd (Reproduced in Southern Cross, Prahran ed., Wed Oct 10, 1979); *2nd row*: Models wearing Le Louvre gowns, courtesy Le Louvre archives; *Third row left*: Miss Darcy Bragg, courtesy Le Louvre archives; *Third row centre*: Portrait of Miss Wightman by Louis Kahan, courtesy Louis and Lily Kahan; *Bottom row left*: Designs for the Hoffman Tales Opera by Miss Wightman and Louis Kahan, Sketch by Louis Kahan; *Bottom row centre*: Portrait of Miss Wightman by Louis Kahan; *Bottom row right*: Ms Barbara Murray-Smith wearing Le Louvre couture, used with permission courtesy Ms Joanna Murray-Smith.and Le Louvre archives. p.**273** Lillian Wightman and client, courtesy Le Louvre archives. p.**276** Featherston chair image, courtesy Gordon Mather.

souvenir *from melbourne*

REFERENCES & FURTHER READING

•*1000 famous Australians*, Rigby, Adelaide, 1978

•Annear, Robyn, *Bearbrass. imagining early Melbourne by*, Mandarin, Port Melbourne, 1995

•Arnold, John, and Morris, Dierdre (eds). *Monash biographical dictionary of 20th century Australia*, Reed Reference Publishing, Port Melbourne, Victoria, c. 1994

•Atkinson, Ann, *The dictionary of famous Australians*, Allen & Unwin, St Leonards, New South Wales, 1992

•*Australian antique collector 1989*, Vol. 37

•*Australian dictionary of biography*, Melbourne University Press, Melbourne; Cambridge University Press, London, New York, 1966–2002

•*Australian dictionary of biography*, Nairn & Serle

•*Australians, a historical library*, Fairfax, Syme & Weldon, Broadway, New South Wales, 1987

•Beilby, Peter (ed.), *Australian TV: the first 25 years* Nelson in association with Cinema Papers, Melbourne, 1981

•*Bert! Bert's own Story*, Gary Sparke & Assoc., Toorak, 1977

•Blake, Les, *Place names of Victoria*, Rigby, Adelaide, 1976

•Borthwick, John, and McGonigal, David (eds). *Melbourne*, photographed by Paul Steel and others. APA Publications, Singapore, c. 1989

•Bouwman, Richard, *Glorious innings: treasures from the Melbourne Cricket Club collection*, Hutchinson, Melbourne, 1987

•Campbell, Alistair H. *John Batman and the Aborigines*, Kibble Books, Malmsbury, Victoria, 1987?

•Carroll, Brian, *Melbourne an illustrated history*, Lansdowne Press, Melbourne, 1972

•Carroll, Brian, *Ned Kelly Bushranger*, Lansdowne Press, New South Wales, 1976

•*The concise encyclopedia of Australia and New Zealand*, Horwitz Grahame Pty Ltd

•Davison, Hirst, Macintyre, *The Oxford companion to Australian history*, Oxford University Press, Melbourne, 1998

•de Courcy, Catherine, *The zoo story*, Penguin, Ringwood, Victoria, 1995

•Dow, David, *Melbourne savages a history of the first 50 years*, Melbourne Savage Club, Melbourne, 1947

•Dunstan, Keith, *The people's ground: the MCG*, 4th ed., Australian Scholarly Publishing, Kew, Victoria, 2000

•Dutton, Geoffrey, *White on black, the Australian Aborigine portrayed in art*, Macmillan, South Melbourne, 1974

•*The economic status of migrants in Australia*, Australian Bureau of Statistics, Queensland, 1990

•Fauchery, Antoine (1823–1861), *Lettres d'un mineur en Australie*. English title: *Letters from a miner in Australia*; translated from French by A. R. Chisholm; drawings by Ron Edwards, Georgian House, Melbourne, 1965

•Finn, Edmond (1817–1898), *The chronicles of early Melbourne, 1835 to 1852: historical anecdotal and personal by 'Garryowen'* Centennial ed., Heritage Publications, Melbourne,1976

•Flower, Cedric, *Picture Book of Australasia When*, Golden Press Ltd, Sydney, 1978

•Goad, Philip, *Melbourne architecture*, The Watermark Press, Balmain, New South Wales, 1998

•*Graham Kennedy's Melbourne*, Thomas Nelson, 1967

•Grant, James , and Serle, Geoffrey, *The Melbourne scene 1803–1956*, first published by Melbourne University Press, Melbourne, 1957, reprinted by Hale & Ironmonger 1978

•Harvey, Anthony, (ed. and illus.), *The Melbourne book*. Introduction by Phillip Adams. Hutchinson of Australia, Richmond, Victoria, 1982

•Horton, Dr David, *Encyclopedia of Aboriginal Australia*, Aborignal Studies Press, Canberra, 1994

•Hugo, Graeme, *Atlas of the Australian people*, Census, Victoria, 1986

•Inson, Graeme, and Ward, Russell, *The glorious years*, Jacaranda, Queensland, 1971

•Johnston, Joseph, *Laughter and the love of friends centenary history of the Melbourne Savage Club 1894–1994*, Melbourne Savage Club, Melbourne, 1994

REFERENCES & FURTHER READING

•Letters from Victorian pioneers: a series of papers on the early occupation of the colony, the aborigines, etc., addressed by Victorian pioneers to His Excellency Charles Joseph La Trobe, Esq.,Lieutenant-Governor of the colony of Victoria, edited for the Trustees of the Public Library by Thomas Francis Bride, published for the Trustees of the Public Library by Robt. S. Brain, Govt. Printe, Melbourne, 1898

•*The life and adventures of William Buckley*, published by John Morgan, Tasmania, 1852, reprinted by Ares Books, Sydney, 1996

•Longmire, Anne, *St Kilda: the show goes on: the history of St Kilda. Volume III, 1930 to July 1983*, N.S. Hudson Publishing, Hawthorn, Victoria, 1989

•McColl Jones, Mike, *And now here's*, Aerospace Publications, 1999

•McColl Jones, Mike, *My funny friends*, Richmond Books, Melbourne, 1979

•*Made in Australia*, William Heineman – Watermark, Sydney, 1986

•Mancini, A., and Hibbins, G. M., (eds). *Running with the ball: football's foster father*, Lynedoch Publications, Melbourne, 1987

•Marshall, Alan, *The Gay Provider, The Myer Story*, Cheshire, Melbourne, 1961

•Mürger, Henry, (1822–1861) *Scènes de la vie de bohème*. English title: *Vie de bohème*; translated from French by Norman Cameron, Hamish Hamilton, London, 1949

•Panda, *Surviving fame memoirs of a TV princess*, Spectrum Publications, Melbourne, 2001

•Priestley, Susan, *South Melbourne: a history*, Melbourne University Press, Carlton, Victoria, 1995

•Priestley, Susan, *The Victorians, making their mark*, Fairfax, Syme & Weldon, New South Wales, 1984

•Reilly, Diane, and Carew, Jennifer, *Sun pictures of Victoria, the Fauchery–Daintree collection 1858* Curry, O'Neill, Ross, Melbourne, 1983 (State Library of Victoria)

•Ridley, Ronald T., *Melbourne's monuments*, Melbourne University Press, Carlton, 1996

•Rienits, Rex and Thea, *A pictorial history of Australia*, Revised ed., Summit Books, Hamlyn New South Wales, 1977

•Ruhen, Olaf, *Port of Melbourne, 1835–1976*, Cassell Australia, Stanmore, New South Wales, 1976

•Sayers, Andrew, *Aboriginal artists of the nineteenth century*, Oxford University Press, Melbourne, 1994

•Serle, Geoffrey, *The Golden Age – A history of the colony of Victoria 1851–1861*

•Statham, Pamela (ed.). *The origins of Australia's capital cities*, Cambridge, England, and Cambridge University Press, Melbourne, 1989

•Stone, Gerald, *Compulsive viewing*, Viking, Melbourne, 2000

•Strutt, William, *Victoria the Golden – scenes, sketches and jottings from nature Melb 1850–1862*, Library Committee, Parliament of Victoria, Melbourne, 1980

•Taylor, Geo, *Making it happen – the rise of Sir Macpherson Robertson*, Robertson and Mullens, Melbourne, 1934

•Tonge, Gera, and Hammond, Stanley, *Public sculpture in Melbourne* [Melbourne: s.n., 1985?]

•Transcription of Robert Buckingham Interview of 19 April 2000 for the Frances Bourke Textile Resource by Sonia Jennings, RMIT Fashion Design Library

•Turnbull, Clive, and Jack, Kenneth (illustrator), *The Melbourne book*, Ure Smith, Sydney, 1948

•U'ren, Nancy, and Turnbull, Noel, *A history of Port Melbourne*, Oxford University Press, Melbourne, 1983

•Vance Wilson, Barbara, *The colonial experience* Oxford University Press, Melbourne, 1990

•Vestey, Pamela, *Melba: a family memoir*, 2nd ed., Pamela Vestey, Melbourne, 2000

•Younger, R. M., *Kangaroo, images through the ages*, Hutchinson Australia, Hawthorn, Victoria, 1988

I would like to thank the following people for their generous help and assistance in the preparation of this book.

The Artists, Estates and Trustees who have allowed use of their artworks, with special thanks to Louis Kahan, Lily Kahan, William Mora Galleries, Mirka Mora, Virginia Edwards, Lauraine Diggins, Albert Tucker Estate, Heide Museum of Modern Art, Brad Hicks, Eric Blaich, Barry Bell, Sam Ritchie, Peter Isaacson, Daryl Wilkinson, Graeme Burfoot, Jude Lengel, Zareh Nalbandian, Wendy Foard, Libby Ross, Ron Robertson-Swann, Michael Mezaros, Louis Laumen, Sean Elliot, Cameron McIndoe.

The Individuals whose time, memories, patience and generosity of spirit has helped me piece together a million details: Philip Brady, Phillip Adams, Tony Sattler, Marie Piccolo, Cole Turnley, Lily Turnley, Georgina Weir, Janet Hogarth-Scott, Baillieu Myer, Margaret Rennie, Trish Palmonari, Kyle Johnston, Harley Metcalfe, Peta & Ed Clark, Bruce Davidson, Beverly Skinner, Beth Klein, Helen Dorian, Chris Erdrich, Jane Stewart, Jim Berg, Len Tregonning, Shannon Faulkhead, Maree Clark, Sandra Smith, Dianne Reilly, Brian Hubber, Simon Warrender, Janine Kirk, Jennie Moloney, Tim Klingender, Kelly Gellatly, Jennifer Ross, William and Lucy Mora, Carmen Greenway, Darryl Rogan, Geoff Enguell, Hanut Dodd, Jane Stewart, Chris Edrich, Genelle Ryan, Snr Sgt. Peter Shaw, Tim Roman, Judy Bell, Judith Henke, David Brodie, Ron Morrison, Margo Radnell, Leanne Mugridge, Maya Kalan, David Studham, Dora Ngov, John Clark, Andrew Paterson, Alison Ware, Eva Janinka, Kay Rowan, Julie Ahern, Tania Twaites, Chong Lim, Vaughn Moncur, Catherine O'Donoghue, Joanna Murray-Smith, Fabrizio Nicolao, Kevin Coote, Kay Ashton, Leanne Hadreck, Jim Oliver, Pam Brajevic, Lyn Elford, Lizzie Crombie, James Allen, Peter Newham, Nannette Fox, Jillian Bowen, Antonia Geddes, Rebeccca Walshe, Tom Beaumont, Katrina Herschell, Kate Bell, Cecily Chun, Cindy Watkins, Paula Fernandez, Rikke Kronberg, Nick Leary, Max de Gasperi, Steven Fehre; Jenny Gibson, Luke Jovanovich, David Preston, Margaret Preston, Silvana Cittadini, Robert Buckingham, Toshi Furuhashi, Chris Connell, Gordon Mather, Jenny Bannister, Liam Lynch, Bill Wright, Stefano Boscutti, Jane Fitzpatrick, Megan Ellis, Simone Wall, Trevor Choy, Tracy O'Shaughnessy.

The Organisations who helped me into Melbourne's stories: State Library of Victoria, National Gallery of Victoria, National Gallery of Australia, Geelong Gallery, Port Melbourne Library, Museum of Victoria, Shrine of Remembrance Trustees, The MCG, The MCC, Information Victoria, Parliament House, Department of Premier and Cabinet, Kulin Nations, Koorie Heritage Trust, Bunjilaka Aboriginal Centre, Immigration Museum, Committee for Melbourne, Melbourne City Council, Melbourne Zoo, Australian Ballet, Melbourne Fashion Festival, Melbourne Performing Arts Museum, Melbourne Water, Bureau of Meteorology, Animal Logic, Film Graphics, Sothebys, ABC TV, Nine Network, Kate's Cottage Glenrowan, Glenrowan Post Office, Chadwick Management, Duet, Robin Gardiner Management, Nannette Fox Artist Representation, Connex, Kraft, Strega Ristorante Italiano, Enoteca Silena, Laurent Boulangerie/Patisserie, Bill Pippis' Clamms Fast Fish, Tony Barbuto's Acland Street Cakes, Akita Japanese Restaurant, Vasiliki, Digital Imaging Group (DIG).

The inspiration, encouragement, patience and love that comes from the four most marvellous Melburnians in the history of the city: Lex, Ginger, Bonny and George. I couldn't have done any of it, without all of you. **Thanks.**

INDEX

INDEX

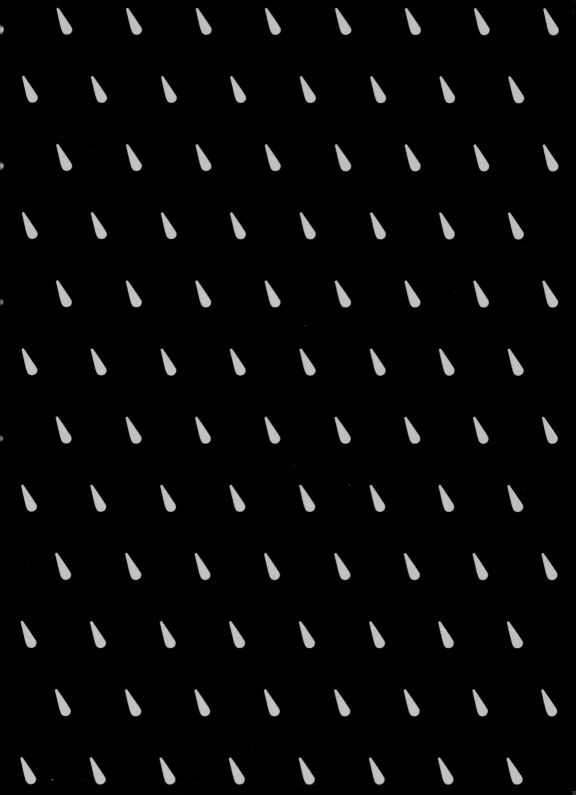

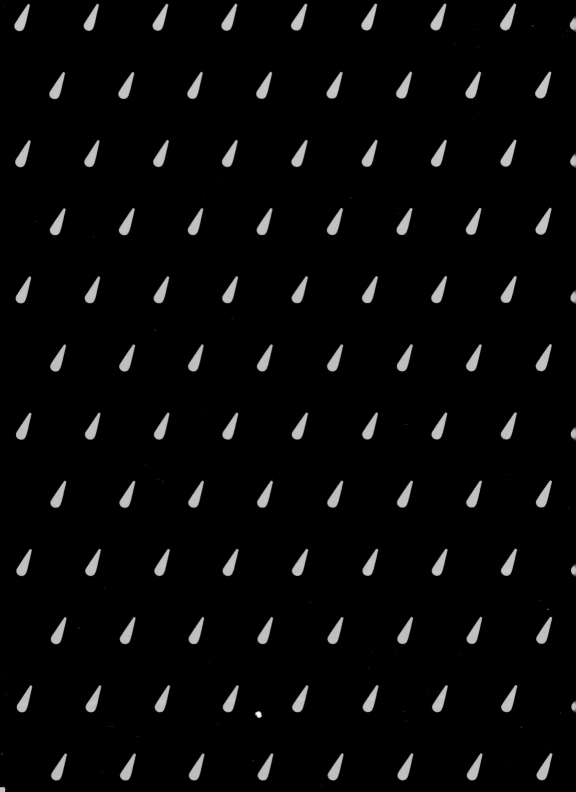